Harcourt Health and Fitness

Teaching Resources
Grade 3

Harcourt
SCHOOL PUBLISHERS

Orlando • Austin • New York • San Diego • Toronto • London

Visit *The Learning Site!*
www.harcourtschool.com

© Harcourt

Contents

Health Resources

School–Home Connection Letters

Writing Models

Contents (Continued)

Organizers

Resources for the Coordinated School Health Program

This directory lists agencies that provide support for the eight different aspects of the Coordinated School Health Program and will aid you in your classroom planning and teaching activities.
While every effort has been made to provide complete and accurate website addresses, the nature of the World Wide Web makes it impossible to follow every link on every site to ensure reliable and up-to-date information. Please use your own discretion about the suitability of the material found on a site, and preview any site to which you refer your students.

Advocates for Youth
1025 Vermont Ave., NW, Suite 210
Washington, DC 20005
Phone: (202) 347-5700
Fax: (202) 347-2263
http://www.advocatesforyouth.org

American Academy of Child & Adolescent Psychiatry
3615 Wisconsin Ave., NW
Washington, DC 20016-3007
Phone: (202) 966-7300
Fax: (202) 966-2891
http://www.aacap.org

American Academy of Pediatrics
141 Northwest Point Blvd.
Elk Grove Village, IL 60007
Phone: (847) 434-4000
Fax: (847) 434-8000
http://www.aap.org

American Association for Active Lifestyles & Fitness
1900 Association Dr.
Reston, VA 22091
Phone: (800) 213-7193
Fax: (703) 476-9527
http://www.aahperd.org/aaalf/aaalfmain.html

American Association for Health Education
1900 Association Dr.
Reston, VA 22091
Phone: (703) 476-3437
Fax: (703) 476-6638
http://www.aahperd.org/aahe/aahemain.html

American Association of School Administrators
1801 N. Moore St.
Arlington, VA 22209
Phone: (703) 528-0700
Fax: (703) 841-1543
http://www.aasa.org

American Cancer Society
1599 Clifton Rd., NE
Atlanta, GA 30329
Phone: (800) 227-2345
Fax: (404) 248-1780
http://www.cancer.org

American College of Sports Medicine
401 W. Michigan St.
Indianapolis, IN 46202-3233
Phone: (317) 637-9200
Fax: (317) 634-7817
http://www.acsm.org

American Dietetic Association
216 W. Jackson Blvd., Suite 800
Chicago, IL 60606
Phone: (312) 899-0040
Fax: (312) 899-1758
http://www.eatright.org

American Federation of Teachers
555 New Jersey Ave., NW
Washington, DC 20001
Phone: (202) 879-4490
Fax: (202) 393-8648
http://www.aft.org

American Medical Association
514 N. State St.
Chicago, IL 60610
Phone: (312) 464-5000
Fax: (312) 464-5842
http://www.ama-assn.org

American Nurses Association
600 Maryland Ave., SW
Suite 100 West
Washington, DC 20024
Phone: (800) 274-4262
Fax: (202) 651-7001
http://www.ana.org

American Psychological Association
750 First St., NE
Washington, DC 20002
Phone: (800) 374-2721
Fax: (202) 336-5962
http://www.apa.org

American Public Health Association
800 I St., NW
Washington, DC 20001-3710
Phone: (202) 777-2742
Fax: (202) 777-2534
http://www.apha.org

American Public Human Services Association
810 First St., NE, Suite 500
Washington, DC 20002
Phone: (202) 682-0100
Fax: (202) 289-6555
http://www.aphsa.org

American Red Cross
8111 Gatehouse Rd.
Jefferson Park
Falls Church, VA 22042
Phone: (703) 206-7180
Fax: (703) 206-7673
http://www.redcross.org

American School Counselor Association
801 N. Fairfax St., Suite 310
Alexandria, VA 22314
Phone: (703) 683-2722
Fax: (703) 683-1619
http://www.schoolcounselor.org

American School Food Service Association
700 South Washington St., Suite 300
Alexandria, VA 22314
Phone: (703) 739-3900
Fax: (703) 739-3915
http://www.asfsa.org

American School Health Association
PO Box 708
Kent, OH 44240
Phone: (330) 678-1601
Fax: (330) 678-4526
http://www.ashaweb.org

Association for Supervision & Curriculum Development
1703 North Beauregard St.
Alexandria, VA 22311-1714
Phone: (703) 578-9600
Fax: (703) 575-5400
http://www.ascd.org

Association of Maternal & Child Health Programs
1220 19 St., NW, Suite 801
Washington, DC 20036
Phone: (202) 775-0436
Fax: (202) 775-0061
http://www.amchp.org

Association of State & Territorial Chronic Disease Program Directors
111 Park Place
Falls Church, VA 22046-4513
Phone: (703) 538-1798
Fax: (703) 241-5603
http://www.astcdpd.org

Association of State & Territorial Dental Directors
322 Cannondale Rd.
Jefferson City, MO 65109
Phone: (573) 636-0453
Fax: (573) 636-0454
http://www.astdd.org

Association of State & Territorial Directors of Health Promotion and Public Health Education
750 First St., NE, Suite 1050
Washington, DC 20002
Phone: (202) 312-6460
Fax: (202) 336-6012
http://www.astdhpphe.org

Association of State & Territorial Health Officials
1275 K St., NW, Suite 800
Washington, DC 20005
Phone: (202) 371-9090
Fax: (202) 371-9797
http://www.astho.org

Association of State & Territorial Public Health Nutrition Directors
1015 15 St., NW, Suite 800
Washington, DC 20005
Phone: (202) 408-1257
Fax: (202) 408-1259
http://www.astphnd.org

California Department of Education
Safe and Healthy Kids Program Office
1430 N. Street, Suite 6408
Sacramento, CA 95814
Phone: (916) 319-0920
Fax: (916) 319-0218
http://www.cde.ca.gov/healthykids

California Healthy Kids Resource Center
313 W. Winton Ave., Room 180
Hayward, CA 94544
Phone: (510) 670-4581
Fax: (510) 670-4582
http://www.hkresources.org

Center for School Mental Health Assistance
University of Maryland-Baltimore,
Department of Psychiatry
680 W. Lexington St., 10th Floor
Baltimore, MD 21201-1570
Phone: (410) 706-0980
Fax: (410) 706-0984
http://www.csmha.umaryland.edu/
csmha2001/main.php3

Centers for Disease Control and Prevention (CDC)
1600 Clifton Rd., NE
Atlanta, GA 30333
Phone: (404) 639-3311
http://www.CDC.gov

Communities in Schools, Inc.
227 S. Washington St., Suite 210
Alexandria, VA 22314
Phone: (703) 519-8999
Fax: (703) 519-7213
http://www.cisnet.org

The Council for Exceptional Children
1110 N. Glebe Rd., Suite 300
Arlington, VA 22201-5704
Phone: (703) 620-3660
Fax: (703) 264-9494
http://www.cec.sped.org

Council of Chief State School Officers
One Massachusetts Ave., NW
Suite 700
Washington, DC 20001
Phone: (202) 408-5505
Fax: (202) 408-8072
http://www.ccsso.org

Council of the Great City Schools
1301 Pennsylvania Ave., NW
Suite 702
Washington, DC 20004
Phone: (202) 393-2427
Fax: (202) 393-2400
http://www.cgcs.org

Employee Assistance Professionals Association
2102 Wilson Blvd., Suite 500
Arlington, VA 22201
Phone: (703) 387-1000
Fax: (703) 522-4585
http://www.eap-association.org

Food Research and Action Center
1875 Connecticut Ave., NW,
Suite 540
Washington, DC 20009
Phone: (202) 986-2200
Fax: (202) 986-2525
http://www.frac.org

National Alliance for the Mentally Ill
Colonial Place Three
2107 Wilson Blvd., Suite 300
Arlington, VA 22201
Phone: (703) 524-7600
Fax: (703) 524-9094
http://www.nami.org

National Alliance of Pupil Services Organizations
7700 Willowbrook Rd.
Fairfax Station, VA 22039
Phone: (703) 250-3414
Fax: (703) 250-6324
https://www.socialworkers.org/

National Assembly on School-Based Health Care
666 11th St., NW, Suite 735
Washington, DC 20001
Phone: (888) 286-8727
Fax: (202) 638-5879
http://www.nasbhc.org

National Association for Sport and Physical Education
1900 Association Dr.
Reston, VA 20191-1599
Phone: (703) 476-3410
Fax: (703) 476-8316
http://www.aahperd.org/naspe/naspemain.html

National Association of Community Health Centers
1330 New Hampshire Ave., NW
Suite 122
Washington, DC 20036
Phone: (202) 659-8008
Fax: (202) 659-8519
http://www.nachc.org

National Association of County & City Health Officials
1100 17th St., NW, 2nd Floor
Washington, DC 20036
Phone: (202) 783-5550
Fax: (202) 783-1583
http://www.naccho.org

National Association of Elementary School Principals
1615 Duke St.
Alexandria, VA 22314
Phone: (703) 684-3345
Fax: (703) 518-6281
http://www.naesp.org

National Association of Health & Fitness
201 S. Capitol Ave., Suite 560
Indianapolis, IN 46225
Phone: (317) 237-5630
Fax: (317) 237-5632
http://www.physicalfitness.org

National Association of Leadership for Student Assistance Programs
PO Box 335
Bedminster, PA 18910
Phone: (215) 795-2119
Fax: (215) 795-0822

National Association of School Nurses
PO Box 1300
Scarborough, ME 04074-1300
Phone: (207) 883-2117
Fax: (207) 883-2683
http://www.nasn.org

National Association of School Psychologists
4340 East West Hwy., Suite 402
Bethesda, MD 20814
Phone: (301) 657-0270
Fax: (301) 657-0275
http://www.nasponline.org

National Association of Social Workers
750 First St., NE, Suite 700
Washington, DC 20002-4241
Phone: (202) 408-8600
Fax: (202) 336-8310
http://www.naswdc.org

National Association of State Boards of Education
277 S. Washington St., Suite 100
Alexandria, VA 22314
Phone: (703) 684-4000
Fax: (703) 836-2313
http://www.nasbe.org

National Association of State NET Program Coordinators
200 W. Baltimore St.
Baltimore, MD 21201
Phone: (410) 767-0222
Fax: (410) 333-2635

National Coalition for Parent Involvement in Education
3929 Old Lee Hwy., Suite 91-A
Fairfax, VA 22030-2401
Phone: (703) 359-8973
Fax: (703) 359-0972
http://www.ncpie.org

National Coalition of Chapter 1 and Title 1 Parents
Edmonds Schools Building
9th and D Sts., NE, Room 201
Washington, DC 20002
Phone: (202) 547-9286
Fax: (202) 547-2813
http://www.nctic1p.org/

National Conference of State Legislatures
1560 Broadway, Suite 700
Denver, CO 80202
Phone: (303) 830-2200
Fax: (303) 863-8003
http://www.ncsl.org

National Council of Churches
475 Riverside Dr.
New York, NY 10115
Phone: (212) 870-2297
Fax: (212) 870-2030
http://www.ncccusa.org

National Council of LaRaza
1111 19th St., NW, Suite 1000
Washington, DC 20036
Phone: (202) 785-1670
Fax: (202) 776-1792
http://www.nclr.org

National Education Association
1201 16th St., NW
Washington, DC 20036
Phone: (202) 883-4000
Fax: (202) 822-7775
http://www.nea.org

National Environmental Health Association
720 South Colorado Blvd., Suite 970-S
Denver, CO 80246
Phone: (303) 756-9090
Fax: (303) 691-9490
http://www.neha.org

National Federation of State High School Associations
PO Box 690
Indianapolis, IN 46206
Phone: (317) 972-6900
Fax: (317) 822-5700
http://www.nfhs.org

National Middle School Association
4151 Executive Parkway, Suite 300
Westerville, OH 43081
Phone: (800) 528-6672
Fax: (614) 895-4750
http://www.nmsa.org

National Network for Youth
1319 F St., NW, Suite 401
Washington, DC 20004
Phone: (202) 783-7949
Fax: (202) 783-7955
http://www.nn4youth.org

National Peer Helpers Association
PO Box 2684
Greenville, NC 27834
Phone: (877) 314-7337
Fax: (919) 522-3959
http://www.peerhelping.org

The National PTA
330 N. Wabash Ave., Suite 2100
Chicago, IL 60611-3690
Phone: (312) 670-6782
Fax: (312) 670-6783
http://www.pta.org

National Safety Council
1121 Spring Lake Dr.
Itasca, IL 60143-3201
Phone: (630) 285-1121
Fax: (630) 285-1315
http://www.nsc.org

National School Boards Association
1680 Duke St.
Alexandria, VA 22314
Phone: (703) 838-6722
Fax: (703) 683-7590
http://www.nsba.org

National Urban League
120 Wall St., 8th Floor
New York, NY 10005
Phone: (212) 558-5300
Fax: (212) 344-5332
http://www.nul.org

National Wellness Association
PO Box 827
Stevens Point, WI 54481-0827
Phone: (715) 342-2969
Fax: (715) 342-2979
http://www.nationalwellness.org

President's Council for Physical Fitness and Sports
Hubert H. Humphrey Building
200 Independence Ave., SW, Room 738H
Washington, DC 20201
Phone: (202) 690-9000
Fax: (202) 690-5211
http://www.fitness.gov

Public Education Network
601 13th St., NW, Suite 900 North
Washington, DC 20005
Phone: (202) 628-7460
Fax: (202) 628-1893
http://www.publiceducation.org

Public Risk Management Association
1815 N. Fort Meyer Dr., Suite 102
Arlington, VA 22209
Phone: (703) 528-7701
Fax: (703) 528-7966
http://www.primacentral.org

Society for Adolescent Medicine
1916 Copper Oaks Circle
Blue Springs, MO 64015
Phone: (816) 224-8010
Fax: (816) 224-8009
http://www.adolescenthealth.org

Society for Nutrition Education
1001 Connecticut Ave., NW, Suite 528
Washington, DC 20036-5528
Phone: (202) 452-8534
Fax: (202) 452-8536
http://www.sne.org

Society for Public Health Education, Inc.
750 First St., NE, Suite 910
Washington, DC 20002-4242
Phone: (202) 408-9804
Fax: (202) 408-9815
http://www.sophe.org

Society of State Directors of Health, Physical Education, and Recreation
1900 Association Dr.
Reston, VA 21091-1599
Phone: (703) 476-3402
Fax: (703) 476-9527
http://www.thesociety.org

State Directors of Child Nutrition
C/O ASFSA
700 S. Washington St., Suite 300
Alexandria, VA 22314
Phone: (703) 739-3900
Fax: (703) 739-3915
http://www.asfsa.org

Wellness Councils of America
9802 Nicholas St., Suite 315
Omaha, NE 68114
Phone: (402) 827-3590
Fax: (402) 827-3594
http://www.welcoa.org

Diseases and Disorders: Background, Symptoms, and Classroom Implications

The following information about various communicable and noncommunicable diseases and disorders is provided for your reference. Background information, signs/symptoms, and school or classroom implications are given for each disease. Consult your school nurse or another medical authority if you have any questions or concerns about the health of your students.

Communicable Diseases and Disorders	Noncommunicable Diseases and Disorders
Chicken Pox (Varicella)	Anorexia Nervosa
Colds	Anthrax
Conjunctivitis (Pinkeye)	Appendicitis
Fifth Disease	Asthma
Hepatitis (Viral)	Bronchitis (Asthmatic or Allergic)
Human Immunodeficiency Virus (HIV) Infection and Acquired Immunodeficiency Syndrome (AIDS)	Cerebral Palsy (CP)
	Diabetes
	Down Syndrome
Impetigo	Epilepsy (Seizure Disorder)
Influenza	Hearing Loss
Measles (Rubella, or German Measles)	Heart Disorders
	Hemophilia (Bleeding Disorder)
Measles (Rubeola)	Leukemia
Mononucleosis (Mono)	Lyme Disease
Mumps	Muscular Dystrophy
Pediculosis (Lice)	Peptic Ulcer
Ringworm (Tinea)	Reye's Syndrome
Scabies	Rheumatic Fever
Smallpox	Rheumatoid Arthritis
Staphylococcal Infections (Staph)	Scoliosis
Strep Throat	Sickle-Cell Anemia
Sudden Acute Respiratory Syndrome (SARS)	Sty
	Tendonitis
Tonsillitis	Tetanus (Lockjaw)
Tuberculosis (TB)	Vision Disorders
	West Nile Virus

Communicable Diseases and Disorders

Infectious conditions, whether communicable among humans or noncommunicable, are receiving more medical and media attention. While much conversation is about agents that might be adapted to hurt or threaten groups, e.g., inhalation anthrax or smallpox, there is much more occurring with "emerging" and re-emerging infections. Several factors are involved: global work that exposes people to new infectious agents; intercontinental travel of people and transportation of animals that harbor infection or objects and insects that can transmit disease (vectors); population increases and crowding; public health and laboratory tests that can identify new organisms and give more specific reasons for illnesses; disrupted habitats (irrigation, deforestation) that allow organisms to jump to another species of animal; contaminated water as breeding ground for organisms; food preparation and distribution across the world; lagging vaccination rates; unrecognized "old" contagious conditions like whooping cough and tuberculosis; microbe resistance to drugs and pesticides; and fewer public health resources for malaria.

Chicken Pox (Varicella)

Background: Chicken pox (varicella) is caused by the varicella zoster virus. This virus can become dormant in nerve cells and later re-activate as shingles. Chicken pox is a relatively mild disease in children without other chronic conditions. However, Reye's syndrome, which can have serious results, is often preceded by salicylate (aspirin) use in viral illnesses such as chicken pox (see "Reye's syndrome" under "Noncommunicable Diseases and Disorders"). A vaccine is available for children between ages 12 and 18 months or older children who have not had varicella.

Symptoms: mild headache and moderate fever, a rash progressing to itching fluid-filled blisters, which then scab and crust over

Classroom Implications: Chicken pox is highly contagious and is spread by direct contact with blister fluid and through nasal discharge. Students may return to school when all the blisters have crusted over. Some may have complications such as pneumonia or secondary skin infection which delay their return.

Colds

Background: Colds are caused by viruses. More than a hundred such viruses have been found to produce the inflammatory reactions associated with colds. Therefore, colds can occur as many as four or five times a year. The key factor is exposure to an infected person. Being chilled does not cause a cold but may lower resistance to developing the disease after exposure.

Symptoms: a tickling sensation in the nose and throat, bouts of sneezing, watery nasal discharge, dulled senses of taste and smell, body aches, a cough, slight fever

Classroom Implications: Because cold and influenza viruses are highly infectious, a child with a "blossoming" cold (fever, cough, sneezes) should probably not be in school. However, many students attend school while recovering. Reinforcing hygiene with students, such as washing the hands regularly and covering the mouth with disposable tissue when coughing or sneezing, may limit the spread. Remember that a student with a fever/cold does not function at his or her best.

Conjunctivitis (Pinkeye)

Background: Conjunctivitis can be caused by viruses, bacteria, or allergies. Conjunctivitis is an inflammation of the membrane that covers the cornea or sclera (the white of the eye). Usually the condition is self-limiting. Viral pinkeye is contagious but there is no anti-viral treatment.

Symptoms: pink or red sclera, possibly discharge or crust on the eyelids, itching

Classroom Implications: Viral conjunctivitis is more contagious than bacterial. A student suspected of having pinkeye should be referred to the school nurse. Students should keep their hands clean, not share eye makeup (older girls), and not share face cloths with anyone who has pinkeye.

Fifth Disease

Background: Fifth disease is a mild illness caused by a virus (human parvovirus B19) usually during elementary school age years. If a woman gets the disease during pregnancy, it can infect the unborn child and, in rare cases, cause complications or death to the fetus. The virus is most likely spread by direct contact with saliva or nasal discharge.

Symptoms: begins with signs of a cold but develops a light red "lacy" rash that tends to come and go on the face, the trunk, and the arms and legs. In adults, joint swelling and pain can also occur.

Classroom Implications: Fifth disease is contagious before the rash appears, so it is often not diagnosed until children are no longer contagious. Children are not usually out of school unless running a fever. A pregnant teacher should discuss exposure with her doctor.

Hepatitis (Viral)

Background: Hepatitis is inflammation of the liver. Different viruses are known to cause some cases of viral hepatitis. They are named hepatitis A, B, C, D, and E viruses. All of them cause short-term, viral hepatitis. Hepatitis B, C, and D viruses can also cause chronic hepatitis, in which the infection is sometimes lifelong. Hepatitis A and E are spread through fecal contamination of water and food. Hepatitis B is spread through blood and certain body secretions, such as by sexual activity, blood exposure during childbirth, and the sharing of used needles for tattoos or drug use. Hepatitis C, the most common form, is spread by infected blood, less often by sexual activity or childbirth. Vaccines are available for hepatitis A and hepatitis B. Hepatitis D can occur in persons with hepatitis B.

Symptoms: nausea, vomiting, fever, loss of appetite during the early phase; jaundice, characterized by dark urine and light-color stools (feces) followed by yellowing of the body surfaces and the whites of the eyes (after three to ten days). Young children may have no signs of illness.

Classroom Implications: Though viral hepatitis resolves within weeks, it is a serious illness. General school exposure does not merit immune globulin. If more than one student in a class contracts hepatitis A, it may be prudent to ask about immune globulin for close contacts in the class. These injections provide some short-term protection against the virus. Good personal hygiene, such as washing hands carefully after changing diapers or helping younger children in the toilet, prevents the spread of the disease and should be emphasized. A student who misses school because of hepatitis will likely require home teaching until recovery is complete.

Human Immunodeficiency Virus (HIV) Infection and Acquired Immunodeficiency Syndrome (AIDS)

Background: HIV is the virus that causes AIDS. Most people with HIV infection develop AIDS.

The virus attacks the body's immune system, and infected people become susceptible to a variety of diseases that are usually not serious threats to people with normal immune systems. The AIDS diagnosis is determined by the presence of these infections and by blood tests. HIV is transmitted through contact with specific body fluids, including blood, semen, and vaginal secretions. It is not spread through the air, water, food, eating utensils, tears, sweat, or skin-to-skin contact. Early diagnosis and new drug treatments may interfere with the virus replication and reduce the risk of developing life-threatening infections.

Symptoms: nonspecific symptoms such as swollen lymph glands, loss of appetite, chronic diarrhea, weight loss, fever and fatigue; secondary viral and bacterial infections and cancers such as Kaposi's sarcoma

Classroom Implications: Most people can avoid exposure to HIV by avoiding risky behaviors such as unprotected sex and the sharing of needles. District health services policy should include guidelines to prevent exposure to body secretions, e.g., access to latex or vinyl gloves when assisting in first aid or direct health care.

Impetigo

Background: Impetigo is a skin infection seen mostly in children. It is usually caused by strains of streptococcal or staphylococcal bacteria. The infection usually appears on the fingers or face and is treated with antibiotics.

Symptoms: small blisters with pus; itchy, weeping sores that develop yellow, honey-colored crusts

Classroom Implications: Impetigo may be spread by direct contact. Students who have unexplained sores should be referred to the school nurse. Untreated lesions may cause scarring. Secondary infections in other parts of the body are possible. Students should be reminded to wash their hands and keep their fingernails clean. Sores should be lightly covered while under treatment to limit scratching or exposure to others.

Influenza

Background: The most frequent cause is the influenza A virus. It is spread by person-to-person contact and by droplets that become airborne because of coughing, sneezing, or talking. Major epidemics occur about every three years and affect persons of all ages. Influenza is most prevalent in school children. The very young, the aged, and persons with a chronic condition such as asthma, sickle-cell anemia, or diabetes are at the greatest risk of developing complications. Each year a vaccine is formulated to protect against the flu viruses expected to circulate the following winter. Those at greatest risk of complications from the virus should be among the first to receive the vaccine.

Symptoms: chills, fever, body aches and pains, headache, sore throat, cough, fatigue

Classroom Implications: Influenza is a self-limiting disease, with acute illness lasting for two to three days. Weakness and fatigue may persist for several days or occasionally for weeks. When a student returns to class after a bout with influenza, he or she may temporarily lack the ability to concentrate.

Measles (Rubella, or German Measles)

Background: Rubella is caused by a virus and is spread through personal contact and through airborne droplets. Rubella is milder and less contagious than rubeola, another type of measles. However, a pregnant woman who contracts rubella in early pregnancy risks serious injury to the fetus.

Symptoms: a rash that eventually covers the body, lasting about three days; mild fever; tenderness and swelling of the lymph nodes at the back of the neck

Classroom Implications: Prevention of rubella is a health priority because of the high risk during pregnancy. Children may be vaccinated between 12 and 15 months of age with a combination measles-mumps-rubella (MMR) vaccine and given a booster after age 4 years.

Measles (Rubeola)

Background: Rubeola is caused by a virus that is spread by nose, throat, and mouth droplets. It is most contagious two to four days before the rash begins and during the acute phase. Children should be vaccinated against rubeola. The recommended age for inoculation is between 12 and 15 months with a booster after age 4 years or by age 12 years if not done previously. The combined measles-mumps-rubella (MMR) vaccine is used.

Symptoms: high fever followed by hacking cough, sneezing, runny nose, redness of the eyes, sensitivity to light, a rash beginning at the face and moving down

Classroom Implications: About 20 percent of measles cases develop complications such as ear infections, pneumonia, or even encephalitis with lasting effects. All rubeola cases should be reported to the health authorities.

Infectious Mononucleosis (Mono)

Background: Infectious mononucleosis is caused by the Epstein-Barr virus, which is one of the herpes group of viruses. Mono is often called the "kissing disease," because it is spread by close contact with infected saliva. Mono is not very contagious. It may be positively diagnosed by a blood test.

Symptoms: fatigue, headache, chills, followed by high fever, sore throat, swelling of the lymph nodes. Enlargement of the spleen occurs in some.

Classroom Implications: Infection with the Epstein-Barr virus occurs commonly in children but often goes unrecognized, as it resembles a bad cold. Infectious mononucleosis, as described above, is predominantly more serious for adolescents and young adults. Symptoms can last weeks, and a variety of complications can occur. Many students with mono are out of school a long time and may be easily fatigued when allowed to return, which should be taken into consideration.

Mumps

Background: Mumps is caused by a virus that is spread by droplet infection or by materials that have been in contact with infected saliva. The virus predominantly affects the parotid salivary glands, which are located in the cheek area, in front of the ears. When infected, these glands swell, giving the person a chipmunk-like appearance. Occasionally, the salivary glands under the tongue become involved, and the neck area may swell.

Symptoms: chills, headache, loss of appetite, fever, pain when chewing or swallowing

Classroom Implications: Children may be vaccinated against mumps between ages 12 and 15 months with a booster after age 4 years (before entering school). The vaccine is usually given in a combined form with the measles and rubella vaccines. All mumps cases should be reported to the proper health authorities.

Pediculosis (Lice)

Background: Lice are small parasitic insects. Three types of lice are known to live on a human host. Crab lice *(Phthirus pubis)* are usually transmitted by very close contact, such as during sex or sharing a bed or towel. Body lice *(Pediculus humanus corporis)* are uncommon under good hygienic conditions. Head lice *(Pediculus humanus capitis)* are transmitted by personal contact: by contact with an infested person (contact is common during play at school and at home at slumber parties, during sports activities, at camp, or on a playground); by wearing infested clothing, such as hats, scarves, coats, sports helmets, or hair ribbons; by using infested combs, brushes, or towels; by lying on a bed, couch, pillow, carpet, or stuffed animal that has recently been in contact with an infested person.

Head lice invade the scalp but can also move to the eyebrows, eyelashes, and other facial hair. The lice lay eggs, called nits, which are grayish white and can be seen adhering to the hair shafts. The nits mature in three to fourteen days.

Symptoms: itching, white nits (eggs) that tightly adhere to the hair shafts

Classroom Implications: Teachers should reinforce prevention habits and limit "head-to-head" group work as well as observe for possible signs, e.g., scratching. If a student in class has lice, other students should be discreetly checked with a hand lens by a person trained to identify lice and nits. The lice can be killed with specially medicated shampoo or creams. Parents/caretakers should be advised to remove the nits to prevent re-infestation. Students should be welcomed back in the classroom following effective treatment.

Ringworm (Tinea)

Background: Ringworm is an infection caused by any of a number of fungi that invade only the dead tissue (keratin) of skin, hair or nails. Infection by a certain fungus can produce raised rings on the skin (hence the name *ringworm*). However, other fungi cause different signs. The various fungi attack specific areas of the body.

Symptoms: slowly spreading, scaly, ring-shaped spots on the skin (ringworm of the body, *tinea corporis*); scaling lesions between the toes ("athlete's foot," *tinea pedis*); thickened, lusterless nails with a darkened appearance (ringworm of the nails, *tinea unguium*); small, scaly lesions on the scalp and semibald, grayish patches with broken, lusterless hairs (ringworm of the scalp, *tinea capitis*)

Classroom Implications: The most common types of ringworm are "athlete's foot" and ringworm of the scalp. Athlete's foot is often spread at swimming pools and in showers, locker rooms, and other such wet facilities. Ringworm of the scalp mainly affects children. If this condition is suspected, a student should immediately be referred to the school nurse. Scalp ringworm requires oral prescribed medication to penetrate the hair follicles.

Scabies

Background: Scabies is an infectious parasitic skin infection caused by the itch mite *(Sarcoptes scabiei)*. Pregnant female mites tunnel into the skin and deposit their eggs. The larvae hatch after a few days and group around the hair follicles. Itching is due to hypersensitivity to the parasites' waste products. Scabies is transmitted through prolonged, not casual, skin-to-skin contact, often infecting entire households. It can be spread through shared clothing or bedding.

Symptoms: intense itching; burrows (fine, wavy, dark lines with small pimple-like lesions at the open ends) occurring commonly between the fingers; burrows also occurring on the insides of the wrists and in skin folds on the abdomen and elbows

Classroom Implications: Suspected scabies needs to be referred to health professionals and treated immediately. Prescribed lotions are necessary and the student may also have medication to relieve itching, which can last a month after treatment while dead skin and mites are shed.

Smallpox

Background: Smallpox is a highly contagious disease that was eliminated in the world in 1977. Vaccination was no longer indicated and the vaccine can have serious side effects. There is some concern that the smallpox virus could be used as a weapon of bioterrorism. There is a smallpox preparedness program to protect Americans against smallpox as a biological weapon. This program includes training teams to respond to a smallpox attack. Healthcare and public health workers are being vaccinated in order to care for and vaccinate others in the event of an outbreak. There is enough smallpox vaccine to vaccinate everyone who would need it.

Symptoms: The incubation period for smallpox is from 7 to 17 days following contact with the virus. Symptoms include high fever, fatigue, headache, and backache. A rash follows in 2 to 3 days. The rash begins as a flat red spot that becomes filled with pus and then begins to crust early in the second week. Scabs form and then fall off after 3 to 4 weeks.

Classroom Implications: Smallpox is spread from person to person by infected droplets of saliva. Persons are most contagious during the first week of illness but may be contagious during the entire period of illness. There is no cure for smallpox, but if the vaccine is given within 4 days of exposure to the virus, it can lessen the severity of the illness or even prevent it.

Staphylococcal Infections (Staph)

Background: Staphylococcal bacteria are commonly found on the skin of healthy people. Those who are hospitalized or work in hospitals have a slightly higher incidence of penicillin-resistant strains. Staph food poisoning is caused by the toxin produced by the staphylococci in contaminated food.

Symptoms: General: fever, headache; Skin: boils, abscesses, skin lesions with pus (impetigo); Food: vomiting

Classroom Implications: All staph infections should be treated promptly by a health professional. Suspect food poisoning when a number of people develop vomiting within hours of eating a food in common, often involving improperly prepared or stored products. Report names, symptoms and food(s) eaten, because staph is just one of the possible culprits.

Strep Throat

Background: Strep throat is caused by one form of streptococcal bacterium. A throat culture can confirm the presence of streptococcal bacteria.

Symptoms: sudden fever and headache, sore, beefy-red throat, nausea or vomiting, swollen neck "glands"; inflamed tonsils with thin white patches on tonsils. Cases that include a rash that is due to a toxin produced by the strep bacteria are called scarletina or scarlet fever.

Classroom Implications: Complications of strep throat can be life-threatening. Rheumatic fever with joint or heart disease or a kidney complication may develop in a small percentage of cases. Therefore, it is very important that students who show symptoms of the disease be evaluated. Any student with fever and sore throat without a cough, laryngitis, or stuffy nose should be suspect.

Sudden Acute Respiratory Syndrome (SARS)

Background: This unusual pneumonia is believed to be caused by a virus in the coronavirus family that exists in wild animals used for food in China. With laboratory advances, the cause of SARS was determined within three months of the early cases—great progress compared to the four years it took to identify HIV.

Symptoms: After 2 to 7 (up to 10) days from exposure, an ill person has fever (over 100°), headache, muscle aches, dry cough, and difficulty breathing.

Classroom Implications: With travel restrictions, young students are unlikely to be exposed. Travelers, family, or health workers exposed to infected persons must stay home for a 10-day "health watch" to monitor for symptoms. Infection control includes standard precautions (hand washing) and air precautions (surgical mask for the patient, air filtration in hospitals) with patients with symptoms and exposure. This is a topic that can be used to encourage students to apply the "disease detective" work of epidemiology to an array of health conditions.

Tonsillitis

Background: Tonsillitis is an acute inflammation of the tonsils, often caused by viruses or common bacteria.

Symptoms: sore throat and pain, especially upon swallowing; fever, headache, vomiting, white patches on the tonsils

Classroom Implications: Repeated tonsillitis may cause frequent absences pending medical evaluation. When students return to school after tonsillectomies, there are usually few restrictions on their activity.

Tuberculosis (TB)

Background: Tuberculosis is an acute or chronic disease caused by a rod-shaped bacterium. TB is primarily a pulmonary disease but can strike other organs and tissues, such as bones. Infection usually occurs after exposure from inhaling infectious droplets. The bacteria settle in the lower or middle section of the lungs and multiply. The body's immune system then fights the disease, producing antibodies against it. Infection may continue to be contained without disease developing. The bacteria may reactivate in persons with lowered resistance due to other chronic conditions. TB exposure is detected by the tuberculin skin test (PPD), and disease is determined by lab tests and a chest X–ray.

Symptoms: fever, body aches, chronic cough that expels sputum

Classroom Implications: In the United States TB has reemerged as a serious public health problem, affecting low income groups that live in close quarters and persons who do not get tested or who do not complete treatment. Drug-resistant cases of TB have also increased dramatically because of incomplete treatment. TB is primarily an airborne disease. Children do not cough deeply enough to spread TB bacteria if they have an infection. Public health officials hire staff to ensure that some infected persons complete their antibiotic treatment to avoid more drug-resistance and spread to others.

Noncommunicable Diseases and Disorders

Anorexia Nervosa

Background: Anorexia nervosa is a psychological condition, an eating disorder that is usually most common among adolescent girls. The disease is characterized by a distorted concept of body image and involves extreme weight loss. Many people with the disorder look emaciated but are convinced they are overweight. Bulimia nervosa is a variant of anorexia nervosa. It is characterized by eating binges followed by purges. Purging may involve vomiting, abusing laxatives or diuretics, taking enemas, exercising obsessively, or a combination of these. As body fat decreases, the menstrual cycle is interrupted.

Symptoms: rapid weight loss, change in eating habits, obsession with exercise to lose weight, increased use of laxatives, depressed mental state, cessation of menstruation, sores around the mouth and dental disease from forced vomiting

Classroom Implications: Eating disorders such as anorexia nervosa and bulimia nervosa may occur in varying severity. They are more successfully treated when diagnosed early. Many cases have been discovered by teachers who have made appropriate referrals. Students with eating disorders need the emotional support of their teachers. Efforts to enhance realistic body image and self-concept in the classroom contribute toward treatment goals.

Anthrax

Background: Anthrax is a noncommunicable infectious disease usually found in cloven-hoofed animals. It can also infect humans. Anthrax infection takes one of three possible forms. They are inhalation, cutaneous, and gastrointestinal. Inhalation anthrax involves inhaling *Bacillus anthracis*. This is the most serious form of infection. Cutaneous, or skin infection, involves transmission through a cut or rash on the skin. This is the least serious form of infection but has been around for centuries. Gastrointestinal infection occurs when infected meat is ingested. Between January 1955 and December 1999, there were 236 reported cases of anthrax in the United States. Most of those cases were cutaneous and occurred among persons who worked with contaminated animal products. Anthrax has been used as an agent of bioterrorism within the United States. A vaccine is available for the prevention of anthrax infection. Antibiotic treatment is available for persons who have been exposed to anthrax or who have developed the disease.

Symptoms: Inhalation: sore throat, mild fever, muscle aches, and general malaise. Respiratory failure, shock, and meningitis often occur.

Cutaneous: a small pimple that enlarges to an ulcer that is black in the center. Fever, headache, malaise, and swollen lymph nodes can be present.

Gastrointestinal: This results from eating raw or undercooked contaminated meat. There is severe abdominal distress with fever and severe diarrhea.

Classroom Implications: Because anthrax cannot be transmitted from person to person, there is little likelihood that there will be an outbreak in the classroom. However, with anthrax being an agent of bioterrorism, be vigilant with unknown substances that may come from unusual sources. Don't open any packages or mail that may be suspicious. Contact the appropriate authorities if you suspect anthrax contamination.

Appendicitis

Background: Appendicitis is most common in adolescents and young adults but is also a major reason for abdominal surgery in children. The appendix becomes infected with bacteria normally found in the bowel. Continued inflammation may lead to abscess formation, gangrene, and perforation resulting in peritonitis.

Symptoms: steady, localized pain, usually in the lower right abdominal quadrant; constipation that began recently; nausea and vomiting; mild fever; elevated white-blood-cell count

Classroom Implications: A student returning to the classroom after an appendectomy may have restrictions on his or her activity for a time. The student may tire easily the first few days and have difficulty concentrating.

Asthma

Background: Asthma is a chronic reversible airway condition that results in recurring episodes (also called *attacks*) of breathing problems. Episodes can be triggered by upper respiratory infections (colds or flu); hard exercise; laughing or crying hard; allergies to common substances such as animal dander (tiny scales from skin), pollen, or dust; irritants such as cold air, strong smells, and chemical sprays (perfume, paint and cleaning solutions, chalk dust, lawn and turf treatments); weather changes; or tobacco smoke. During an episode the muscles surrounding the bronchial tubes tighten, thus reducing the size of the airway. The allergic response causes mucus production and a resultant productive cough. People with asthma are able to draw air into the lungs through the narrowed airway but are unable to expel carbon dioxide waste out. They may cough, wheeze, gasp for air, and feel that they are suffocating.

Symptoms: wheezing, gasping for air, hacking cough, tightness in the chest, shortness of breath

Classroom Implications: An asthma episode may be compared to taking a deep breath and not being able to let it out. A student having an asthma episode should be reassured that help is on the way. People with asthma are often fearful of the episodes. An episode may occur at any time and may be triggered by emotional strain, physical exertion, or environmental factors. Many students with asthma take prescription prevention (control) and rescue (acute) medicines, which should be available to them when needed. These medicines may cause jitteriness, overactivity, or, rarely, drowsiness. With medical management and monitoring with peak flow meters at home and school, students with asthma usually have few restrictions on activity, except during or following an acute episode.

Bronchitis (Asthmatic or Allergic)

Background: Bronchitis is inflammation of the bronchial tubes. It may develop as a result of an environmental irritant like cigarette smoke or from an upper-respiratory infection. A virus or bacterium invades the area and causes inflammation and increases mucus secretion. A deep, rumbling cough develops. Treatment is directed at drainage and expulsion of the mucus rather than at suppression of the cough.

Symptoms: chills, slight fever, back and muscle pain, sore throat, followed by dry cough and then by a cough that expels mucus

Classroom Implications: Bronchitis is a self-limiting disease in most cases; complete healing usually occurs within a few weeks. The student who has bronchitis, however, may be absent and may require help in making up missed work.

Cerebral Palsy (CP)

Background: Cerebral palsy is a term for a group of non-progressive motor disorders that impair voluntary movement. The various forms of CP are caused by developmental problems or injury to the motor areas of the central nervous system before, during, or soon after birth. Physical therapy helps many people with CP overcome their disabilities.

Symptoms: spasticity of limbs, weakness, limb deformities, speech disorders, involuntary movements, difficulty with fine movements, visual disturbances; commonly accompanied by nerve deafness, mental impairment, or seizure disorders

Classroom Implications: Students with severe CP can be mainstreamed with therapy services and support. In mild forms of CP, the symptoms may be seen only during certain activities, such as running. Students with mild CP have the usual range of intelligence and function in a regular classroom setting. Be aware of the student's particular needs, and include the student in classroom activities. Discussing the disorder with classmates and explaining why the student may sometimes move differently will increase understanding and help eliminate teasing. Drugs can be used to control seizures and muscle spasms; special braces can compensate for muscle imbalance. Surgery and mechanical aids can help to overcome impairments. Counseling and physical, occupational, speech, and behavioral therapy may be included in the student's education plan.

Diabetes

Background: Diabetes is characterized by an increase of sugar (glucose) in the blood, which also spills into the urine. In type 1 diabetes, an autoimmune disorder, cell groups in the islets of Langerhans of the pancreas no longer secrete adequate amounts of the hormone insulin. Insulin is the primary substance that allows the body to utilize sugar. In type 2 diabetes, there is a genetic predisposition to develop diabetes along with significant overweight and low physical activity that interferes with the body's use of available insulin to move sugar into the body cells, especially the muscle and fat tissue cells. There is no known cure but research is exploring pancreas cell transplantation for type 1. Optimal treatment usually consists of regulated insulin replacement (by injection or pump), self-monitoring of blood glucose, daily diet, and exercise.

Symptoms: fatigue, frequent urination, thirst, hunger, weight loss (type 1), infections that do not heal quickly

Classroom Implications: Teachers are often in a position to help identify undiagnosed diabetes. Any changes in bathroom or drinking habits should be investigated. Unexplained weight loss or the inability to concentrate or new irritability should also be suspect. A student with regulated diabetes functions normally in the classroom. If you have a student requiring insulin shots, keep a source of sugar, such as orange juice, available for low insulin (hypoglycemia) episodes. You need to accommodate a student on insulin or oral medications for type 2 diabetes who must have a snack once or twice a day at school, self-check blood glucose non-disruptively in the classroom, self-inject insulin on schedule or as the monitoring results indicate. Physical education and meal/snack time need to be coordinated.

Down Syndrome*

Background: Down syndrome is an inherited condition that is usually associated with an extra chromosome. Fifty percent of infants with the syndrome are born to mothers over the age of 35.

Genetic conditions named for individuals are spelled without 's, as recommended by the American Society of Human Genetics.

Children with Down syndrome have a mean IQ of 50. They usually have small heads and slanted eyes. Life expectancy is normal in the absence of other birth defects, such as heart disease.

Symptoms: placidity, poor muscle tone; slanted eyes, flattened nosebridge; mouth usually held open because of enlarged tongue; short-fingered, broad hands with single crease; feet with a wide gap between the first and second toes

Classroom Implications: Children with Down syndrome often have special education resources to meet their individual needs and group activities such as Special Olympics. But many students are part of the regular classroom community. Their classmates need to understand conditions that make others different. A careful introduction to disabilities is a must for the whole class.

Epilepsy (Seizure Disorder)

Background: Epilepsy, a disorder of the nerve cells in the brain, is characterized by episodes of muscle spasms or strange sensations called seizures. The well-known kinds of generalized seizures are grand mal, petit mal, and psychomotor or temporal lobe. During a seizure, brain impulses become chaotic, causing the person to lose full consciousness and control over body movement.

Symptoms: uncontrollable jerking movements followed by a deep sleep (tonic-clonic seizure or convulsion); momentary cessation of movement (absence seizure); coordinated but strange whole body movements while in altered consciousness (simple partial or complex partial seizure)

Classroom Implications: If a student is known to have seizures, get details about the specific type, medications, and what to expect. In a tonic-clonic seizure, do not attempt to restrain the person. If the student has not fallen, gently move him or her onto the floor and move any obstructions out of the way. Do not place any objects in the student's mouth. A convulsive seizure may be a frightening experience to witness, so offer others a simple explanation and reassurance. Absence seizures, though less dramatic, make the student unresponsive with rapid blinking or other behavior; the student briefly loses consciousness. Anticonvulsive medications have side effects, such as drowsiness or making concentration difficult. Computer screens, video games, and flashing lights have been known to trigger seizures. People with epilepsy follow safety guidelines such as wearing helmets for bike riding or climbing, and swimming only with a life jacket at all times.

Hearing Loss

Background: Many conditions can produce hearing loss. Conduction deafness can be caused by sound waves being blocked by wax or by scars from middle-ear infections. It can also be caused by Eustachian tube dysfunction, middle ear fluid, or fixation of the bones of the middle ear. Most of these conditions can be reversed, and normal hearing can be restored. However, when the auditory nerve is damaged, such as by disease or prolonged loud noise, little can be done.

Symptoms: apparent inattention, frequent asking for repetition of what was said, frequent misunderstanding of verbal directions, failure to respond to normal voices or sounds, cupping of the ear to funnel sounds

Classroom Implications: Students with diagnosed hearing loss may require special seating and aids in the classroom. Some students need to wear one or two hearing aids, which should be explained to the rest of the class. Other amplification aids should be supplied when needed. If you observe changes in any student's ability to hear, make referrals for testing.

Heart Disorders

Background: Many conditions can cause heart disorders. The most common disorders in infancy and early childhood are congenital abnormalities such as valve problems, holes between right and left chambers (septal defects), and failure of an opening between the aorta and the pulmonary artery to close after birth (a condition called patent ductus arteriosus). These conditions can be surgically corrected in most instances. Another type of heart condition is a heart murmur, a series of prolonged heart sounds that can be heard as vibrations. Some murmurs are significant but most are not; they are called functional and usually disappear in time. Some significant murmurs may signal developmental heart-valve abnormalities.

Symptoms: shortness of breath, chest pain, blue tinge to the skin, fatigue, slowing of heartbeat rate, palpitations

Classroom Implications: Children who have had surgical correction for congenital heart disorders usually lead restriction-free lives. Those who have continuing problems or who develop additional problems may have to curtail physical activity, and you may need to make special plans for them. All students should be encouraged to develop good physical fitness habits and healthful eating habits to help reduce the risk for adult causes of heart disease such as high cholesterol.

Hemophilia (Bleeding Disorder)

Background: Hemophilia is one inherited bleeding disorder. Others include von Willebrand and platelet disorders. The person is unable to manufacture certain essential clotting factors and therefore might bleed to death or suffer joint damage if a cut or bruise is left untreated.

Symptoms: serious bleeding or bruising from minor injuries or normally lost tooth or heavy menstrual period

Classroom Implications: Most students who have bleeding disorders can lead normal lives if they are receiving treatment for the missing blood clotting factor. However, you should be aware of this condition and take necessary precautions to prevent injury. First-aid procedures for external and internal bleeding should be reviewed with the school nurse or with a physician. Minor episodes may be treated with a prescribed nasal spray medication.

Leukemia

Background: Leukemia is a cancer of white blood cells that eventually crowd out normal white, red, and platelet blood cells. There are several types of leukemia. Acute lymphoblastic leukemia (ALL) primarily affects children. Acute myeloid leukemia (AML) can occur in people of any age. In all people with leukemia, abnormal white blood cells form in large numbers. In children, the causes are unclear and may include genetic tendencies and conditions such as Down syndrome.

Symptoms: high fever and joint pain; bleeding from the mouth, nose, kidneys, and large intestine; enlarged liver, spleen, and lymph nodes

Classroom Implications: Continual improvement in chemotherapy has made remissions (absences of any signs of the disease) much more common, especially in acute lymphoblastic leukemia. Students undergoing treatment for leukemia may be able to return to school after the acute stage of the disease has been arrested. However, depending on the treatment schedule, they may have to return to the hospital periodically. Every effort to maintain continuity in the classroom for these students should be made. Many of the drugs that are administered cause hair loss, which should be explained to the rest of the class. Sometimes students become frightened by the word cancer, and questions such as "Can I catch it?" "Will he die?" and "Will I die?" may be asked. Dealing with these types of concerns openly and honestly may alleviate fear and anxiety.

Lyme Disease

Background: Lyme disease is caused by a spirochete that is transmitted to humans by deer ticks.

Symptoms: After 3 to 32 days from a tick bite exposure (lasting 12 or more hours), a skin lesion begins as a red spot or bump, but enlarges to look like a "bull's eye." Other signs are flu-like tiredness, chills, muscle and joint pain, and swollen lymph glands. Complications include joint arthritis, Bell's palsy, and heart rate irregularities.

Classroom Implications: Persons conducting school outings in areas infested by ticks should instruct students to wear protective clothing and to check hourly for ticks. Any ticks should be removed with an appropriate technique and the site cleaned.

Muscular Dystrophy

Background: The muscular dystrophies are a group of inherited progressive diseases that produce a breakdown in the muscle fibers, causing increasing weakness and difficulty with movement and breathing. Duchenne muscular dystrophy is the most common form. It occurs in boys 3 to 7 years of age. The disease causes a steady increase in muscle weakness, and most patients use a wheelchair by the age of 10 or 12.

Symptoms: muscle weakness causing a waddling gait, toe-walking, a swaybacked appearance, frequent falls, difficulty in standing up and in climbing stairs

Classroom Implications: Many children with muscular dystrophy, especially the less common, milder forms, are mainstreamed. If one of your students has muscular dystrophy, you need to be aware of his or her specific progression and limitations. Special equipment along with physical and occupational therapy may be needed for instruction and for support. Fostering understanding among classmates is of utmost importance.

Peptic Ulcer

Background: A peptic (stomach) ulcer is a sore or hole in the stomach or the first part of the small intestine (duodenum). It used to be thought that a peptic ulcer was a chronic disease that resulted from the overproduction of gastric juices manufactured by the stomach to break down foods. However, in the mid-1980s it was discovered that most ulcers may be caused by a bacterium, *Helicobacter pylori*. These ulcers can be cured with antibiotics. The course of treatment lasts for two weeks and can permanently cure the ulcer. Peptic ulcers are relatively common among adults, though they do occur in children, even before the age of 10.

Symptoms: a painful burning sensation, usually relieved by meals and occurring at night; nausea and vomiting if the pain is severe; constipation; anemia

Classroom Implications: Students who complain of persistent, localized stomach pain should see a physician. Most often a course of antibiotics will be prescribed.

Reye's Syndrome

Background: The cause of Reye's syndrome is currently unknown. Reye's syndrome (RS) is primarily a children's disease, although it can occur at any age. It affects all organs of the body but is most harmful to the brain and the liver—causing an acute increase of pressure within the brain and, often, massive accumulations of fat in the liver and other organs. The disorder commonly occurs during recovery from a viral infection, although it can also develop 3 to 5 days after the onset of the viral illness (most commonly influenza or chicken pox). The cause of RS remains a mystery. However, studies have shown that using aspirin or salicylate-containing medications to treat viral illnesses increases the risk of developing RS.

Symptoms: uncontrollable nausea and vomiting about the sixth day after a viral infection; noticeable change in mental function; lethargy, mild amnesia, disorientation, agitation, unresponsiveness, coma, seizures, fixed and dilated pupils

Classroom Implications: Parents should be informed of the possible link between aspirin and Reye's syndrome. Some people recover completely, while others may sustain varying degrees of brain damage. The syndrome may leave permanent neurological damage, causing mental retardation or problems with movement.

Rheumatic Fever

Background: Rheumatic fever is a possible secondary complication of a streptococcal infection, especially strep throat. Rheumatic fever is an acute inflammatory reaction to the streptococcal bacterium and can affect one or more major sites, including the joints, the brain, the heart, and the skin. The disease is rare before 4 years of age and uncommon after age 18.

Symptoms: varied symptoms appearing alone or in combination after a severe sore throat: a flat, painless rash, lasting less than a day; painless nodules on the legs; swollen tender joints; recurrent fevers; movement disorders.

Classroom Implications: Since rheumatic fever can develop to varying degrees, the amount of physical restriction depends on the joint and cardiac problems of the individual. Psychological problems have been noted in students who have been restricted from play because they have rheumatic fever. It is important for all parents and school personnel to see that a student with a possible strep infection is treated promptly. Any changes in a student's work habits, appearance, or energy level after a strep infection should be investigated.

Rheumatoid Arthritis

Background: Rheumatoid arthritis is a chronic autoimmune disorder characterized by inflammation of the joints. The immune system, for unknown reasons, attacks a person's own cells inside the joint capsule. White blood cells travel to the synovium and cause a reaction. As rheumatoid arthritis progresses, these abnormal synovial cells destroy the cartilage and bone within the joint. The surrounding muscles, ligaments, and tendons that support and stabilize the joint become weak.

In children the knees, elbows, wrists, and other large joints tend to be affected. This may result in interference with growth and development. In some cases the eyes and heart are affected. Complete remission is more likely in children than in adults.

Symptoms: rash, fever, inflammation of the irises, enlargement of the spleen and lymph nodes; swelling, pain, and tenderness of the involved joints

Classroom Implications: A student with rheumatoid arthritis may be absent frequently because of the chronic, recurring nature of the disease and may need help in keeping up with schoolwork. Stiffness of joints and possible deformities may limit the student's movement. Restrictions on the student's activity can be less burdensome if you explain the situation to the whole class. Emotional support from classmates can contribute to the student's sense of well being. Care usually includes healthy lifestyle (diet, exercise, and rest), stress management, medications for pain and inflammation, and sometimes joint surgery.

Scoliosis

Background: Scoliosis is a lateral curvature of the spine. This disorder occurs most commonly during the adolescent growth period. It is estimated that between 5 and 10 percent of school age children have a single or double spinal curvature in varying degrees. However, only about 2 percent of the cases are significant. The effect of scoliosis depends on its severity, how early it is detected, and treatment adherence. The curve usually does not get worse once the spine has reached full growth. Scoliosis is more common among girls than boys.

Symptoms: unequal shoulder levels, a hunchbacked appearance (kyphosis or C-shaped curve), fatigue or muscle aches in the lower back region, persistent back pain

Classroom Implications: Many states now require scoliosis screening for preadolescent and adolescent students. Treatment of scoliosis may range from monitoring to muscle development exercises, to bracing, or to corrective surgery. Special braces or casts can threaten a teenager's self-concept. Therefore, counseling and support from teachers, parents, and peers are very important in treating a youngster with scoliosis.

Sickle-Cell Anemia

Background: Sickle-cell anemia is an inherited disease that affects African Americans mainly but not exclusively. Anemias are conditions in which the blood is low in red blood cells or in hemoglobin, causing a decrease in the body's ability to transport oxygen to all cells. This disease is named after the abnormal, sickle shape of some red blood cells that was a protective adaptation to fight malaria. Because of their shape these cells are not able to flow easily through the capillaries and tend to jam up around joints and in organs. This inhibiting of blood flow can cause acute pain.

Symptoms: fatigue, painful crises when blood vessels are blocked, yellow skin and eyes (jaundice), enlarged spleen, poor growth and delayed puberty, vision abnormalities

Classroom Implications: Sickle-cell anemia can cause repeated painful crisis situations that may require hospital treatment. A student with the disease may be out of school frequently and will need help in completing schoolwork and maintaining contact with the class. Support students' self-care which includes drinking extra water, pain medicines at school, moderate exercise, diet rich in folic acid, avoiding extreme cold and heat, and avoiding exposure to infections.

Sty

Background: Sties are inflamed hair follicles or glands on the eyelids. They are usually caused by staphylococcal bacteria.

Symptoms: a tiny abcess on the eyelid, redness, tenderness of the eyelid, sensitivity to light, the feeling of having a foreign body in the eye

Classroom Implications: Students who develop sties should be referred to the school nurse and may improve with the application of warm compresses. If not improved in 2–3 days, referral to a physician is indicated. Sties are not contagious.

Tendonitis

Background: Tendonitis is an inflammation of the tendons surrounding various joints (shoulder, elbow, wrist, and knee most often). The inflammation usually results from a joint being forced beyond its normal range of motion or in an abnormal direction. Excessive exercise or repeated injury to a joint may also cause tendonitis. A common form of tendonitis, tennis elbow, results from the excessive rotation of the forearm and hand while playing tennis. The muscles of the forearm are strained, and the inflammation spreads to the elbow.

Symptoms: swelling, local tenderness, disabling pain when the affected joint is moved

Classroom Implications: Students may develop tendonitis from excessive periods of repeated exercise such as pitching a baseball or hitting a tennis ball. Students who spend many hours working the levers of video games may experience tendonitis of the wrist joint. Tendonitis may often be prevented through proper coaching in technique and appropriate periods of rest. Cross-training mixes impact-loading exercise, such as running, with lower-impact exercise, such as biking or swimming. Students who complain of constant, disabling pain in any joint should be referred for medical evaluation.

Tetanus (Lockjaw)

Background: Tetanus is an acute infectious disease caused by a bacterium that produces spores and that can live in an environment without oxygen, namely soil or animal feces. Once the toxin from the bacterium enters the body, it interferes with the central nervous system's ability to transmit impulses correctly. This causes a generalized spasticity and intermittent convulsive movements. Stiffness of the jaw is a classic symptom of tetanus (hence the name lockjaw). The typical route of transmission is through a skin wound, usually a dirty splinter or puncture wound, such as from a knife or nail that has been contaminated with dirt containing the spores. The spores then develop into bacteria that release the toxin. Primary immunization against tetanus begins in infancy with a booster at school age. This is given in the form of a DTaP (diphtheria-tetanus-acellular pertussis) combination vaccine. After that, booster injections should be administered every 10 years lifelong.

Symptoms: stiff jaw muscles and difficulty in swallowing; restlessness and irritability; stiffness in the neck, arms, or legs; headache, fever, sore throat, chills, convulsions

Classroom Implications: Help students clean all wounds promptly and thoroughly to prevent exposure. If a student suffers a deep wound and has not had a tetanus booster within five years, his/her doctor may order a booster within two days. Following first aid, all wounds of concern should be reported to the school nurse for proper evaluation.

Vision Disorders

Background: There are three common eye disorders that produce errors in refraction and that decrease visual acuity. The most common childhood disorder is farsightedness (hyperopia), which interferes with the ability to see clearly things that are nearby. In nearsightedness (myopia) a person is able to see things clearly that are near, but distance vision is impaired. Astigmatism, or distorted vision, occurs when there are defective curvatures of the refractive surfaces of the cornea. Other conditions such as eye muscle imbalance also interfere with clear binocular vision. Young children may suppress poorer vision in one eye and, if not treated, in preschool years may permanently lose the vision in that eye (developing amblyopia).

Symptoms: head tilt, squinting, headaches, eye muscle fatigue, holding reading material unusually close or far away, complaining of not being able to see the board, inability to do fine motor or sport tasks as well as expected for age and overall development.

Classroom Implications: Make sure vision screening and any referrals are completed as soon as possible to limit the risk of amblyopia. Students with undiagnosed eye disorders may have a difficult time with schoolwork. As a teacher you are in an excellent position to note such problems and to make appropriate referrals. Reinforce wearing and care for glasses as prescribed, and refer families that need community resources to get needed glasses (not usually covered by health insurance).

West Nile Virus

Background: The West Nile virus (WNV) was first known in 1937 and is in the family Flavivirus, related to the type that causes St. Louis encephalitis. WNV arrived in the US about 1999 through imported animals and objects. Generally, WNV is spread by the bite of an infected mosquito. Mosquitoes harbor the virus in the salivary glands after feeding on infected birds. Infected mosquitoes can then spread WNV to humans and other animals they bite.

Symptoms: WNV affects the central nervous system. Most people (80 percent) will not show any symptoms. Up to 20 percent will have mild symptoms for a few days, including fever, headache, body aches, nausea, vomiting, and sometimes swollen lymph glands or a skin rash (trunk). About one in 150

people infected with WNV will develop severe illness: high fever, headache, neck stiffness, coma, tremors, convulsions, muscle weakness, vision loss, numbness, and paralysis. These symptoms may last several weeks, and neurological effects may be permanent.

Implications: The best way to avoid WNV is to prevent mosquito bites. School buildings should have good screens on windows and doors. Get rid of mosquito breeding sites by emptying standing water. Drill drainage holes in tire swings so water drains out. Keep children's wading pools empty and on their sides when not being used. During activities, precautions should be taken. When outdoors, use insect repellents containing DEET (N, N-diethyl-meta-toluamide). Wear long sleeves and pants.

School-Home Connection

What We Are Learning About Health

In Chapter 1 of *Harcourt Health and Fitness,* we are learning about

- the major organs and their functions.
- positive health behaviors that help the body during stages of growth.
- communicating to someone when feeling upset or uncomfortable.
- respecting adults, especially seniors.

 Visit **www.harcourtschool.com/health** for links to parent resources.

How You Can Help

Parental involvement in the school environment is part of a coordinated school health plan that includes the home, school, community, and social services. You can support your school through increased communication and by volunteering your time or talents. At home you can support your child's learning by

- discussing the changes your own body went through as you grew.
- encouraging your child to talk to a trusted adult when troubled or upset.
- praising your child for showing respect toward others.

A Family Activity

The body is made up of many different systems. After your child has reviewed this chapter, have him or her list what the different body systems do. He or she can also list what he or she can do to promote the well-being of these systems. Discuss the results.

Body System	Function	Care
Digestive		
Respiratory		
Skeletal		
Muscular		
Nervous		

La escuela y la casa

Nota para los familiares

Lo que estamos aprendiendo acerca de la Salud

En el Capítulo 1 de *Harcourt Health and Fitness* estamos aprendiendo acerca de:

- Los órganos principales del cuerpo humano y su función.
- Los buenos hábitos de salud que contribuyen al crecimiento adecuado.
- Cómo comunicar sentimientos de incomodidad y disgusto.
- El respeto por los adultos, especialmente por las personas de la tercera edad.

 Visite **www.harcourtschool.com/health** para encontrar enlaces con recursos en inglés para los padres.

Cómo puede usted ayudar

La participación familiar en las actividades escolares forma parte de un plan de salud organizado que incluye la casa, la escuela, la comunidad y los servicios sociales. Usted puede apoyar a la escuela manteniendo una buena comunicación y ofreciendo su tiempo y sus talentos como voluntario. En casa, usted puede apoyar el aprendizaje de su hijo(a) haciendo lo siguiente:

- Háblele sobre los cambios que su cuerpo experimentó cuando usted estaba creciendo.
- Anímelo a hablar de sus sentimientos con un adulto de confianza, cuando esté disgustado o molesto.
- Elógielo cuando actúe respetuosamente.

Actividad familiar

El cuerpo humano está integrado por muchos sistemas. Pida a su hijo(a) que repase el contenido de la lección y que luego escriba en la tabla la función de cada uno de los sistemas citados, así como las cosas que puede hacer para mantenerlo sano. Hablen sobre la información de la tabla.

Sistema	Función	Manera de cuidarlo
Digestivo		
Respiratorio		
Óseo		
Muscular		
Nervioso		

© Harcourt

Name _____ Date _____

School-Home Connection

A Note to Family Members

What We Are Learning About Health

In Chapter 2 of *Harcourt Health and Fitness,* we are learning about

- the importance of personal hygiene, from washing hands to taking care of the skin.
- caring for and avoiding problems with the eyes, ears, and nose.
- choosing the correct products to maintain proper hygiene and health.
- showing self-respect through good grooming.

 Visit **www.harcourtschool.com/health** for links to parent resources.

How You Can Help

Parental involvement in the school environment is part of a coordinated school health plan that includes the home, school, community, and social services. You can support your school through increased communication and by volunteering your time or talents. At home you can support your child's learning by

- setting up a schedule for daily hygiene habits.

- discussing the importance or caring for the eyes and ears.

- praising your child's efforts to be personally responsible for good grooming.

A Family Activity

With your child, make an inventory of health care products currently found in your home. What does the table tell you about your family? For example, if your family includes elderly members, then the table might include products for cleaning dentures. If your family includes teenagers, then the chart might have many skin-care products.

Skin	Teeth / Gums	Ears / Hearing	Eyes / Vision

© Harcourt

La escuela y la casa

Nota para los familiares

Lo que estamos aprendiendo acerca de la Salud

En el Capítulo 2 de *Harcourt Health and Fitness* estamos aprendiendo acerca de:

- La importancia de desarrollar buenos hábitos de higiene personal, como lavarse las manos y cuidar de la piel.
- El cuidado de los ojos, los oídos y la nariz.
- Los productos adecuados para la salud y la buena higiene.
- El cuidado e higiene personal como una forma de mostrar respeto a sí mismo.

 Visite **www.harcourtschool.com/health** para encontrar enlaces con recursos en inglés para los padres.

Cómo puede usted ayudar

La participación familiar en las actividades escolares forma parte de un plan de salud organizado que incluye la casa, la escuela, la comunidad y los servicios sociales. Usted puede apoyar a la escuela manteniendo una buena comunicación y ofreciendo su tiempo y sus talentos como voluntario. En casa, usted puede apoyar el aprendizaje de su hijo(a) haciendo lo siguiente:

- Organicen un horario de actividades diarias de higiene.
- Comenten acerca de la importancia de mantener los ojos y los oídos sanos.
- Elógielo cuando se responsabiliza por su cuidado personal.

Actividad familiar

Hagan un inventario de los productos de aseo personal que haya en la casa y llenen la tabla con la información que encuentren. ¿Qué pueden decir sobre los hábitos de su familia? Si hay personas mayores, quizá encontrarán productos para el cuidado de la dentadura postiza. Si hay adolescentes, muy posiblemente habrá limpiadores especiales para la cara.

La piel	Dientes/Encías	Oídos	Ojos

Name _____ Date _____

School-Home Connection

What We Are Learning About Health

In Chapter 3 of *Harcourt Health and Fitness,* we are learning about

- using MyPyramid to make healthful and appropriate food choices.
- accurately reading, understanding, and comparing food labels.
- making responsible decisions about snacks.
- steps to take in choosing healthful foods.

 Visit **www.harcourtschool.com/health** for links to parent resources.

How You Can Help

Parental involvement in the school environment is part of a coordinated school health plan that includes the home, school, community, and social services. You can support your school through increased communication and by volunteering your time or talents. At home you can support your child's learning by

- reviewing MyPyramid together.
- comparing the food labels on products in your home.
- praising your child's efforts to make healthful food choices.

A Family Activity

One way to ensure a healthful diet is to eat three meals a day. In the space provided, ask your child to record what he or she eats on a particular day. Then, use the questions that follow as a springboard for discussing whether or not your child is eating a balanced diet.

What I Ate Today

Breakfast:	
Lunch:	
Dinner:	
Snacks:	

Questions

1. What vegetables and fruits did you eat today?
2. Did you drink low-fat milk or eat yogurt or cheese?
3. Did you have bread, cereal, rice, or pasta?
4. Did you eat meat, fish, dried beans, eggs, or nuts?

© Harcourt

La escuela y la casa

Nota para los familiares

Lo que estamos aprendiendo acerca de la Salud

En el Capítulo 3 de *Harcourt Health and Fitness* estamos aprendiendo acerca de:

- MiPirámide y su utilidad al escoger los alimentos adecuados.
- Cómo entender y comparar la información de las etiquetas de los alimentos.
- Cómo seleccionar los mejores refrigerios.
- Los pasos a seguir cuando se desee escoger alimentos saludables.

 Visite **www.harcourtschool.com/health** para encontrar enlaces con recursos en inglés para los padres.

Cómo puede usted ayudar

La participación familiar en las actividades escolares forma parte de un plan de salud organizado que incluye la casa, la escuela, la comunidad y los servicios sociales. Usted puede apoyar a la escuela manteniendo una buena comunicación y ofreciendo su tiempo y sus talentos como voluntario. En casa, usted puede apoyar el aprendizaje de su hijo(a) haciendo lo siguiente:

- Estudien MiPirámide.
- Lean y comparen la información de las etiquetas de los alimentos que tengan en la casa.
- Elógielo cuando escoja alimentos saludables.

Actividad familiar

Para seguir una dieta saludable debemos tener por lo menos tres comidas diarias. Pida a su hijo(a) que escriba lo que come en el desayuno, el almuerzo y la cena en un día cualquiera, en la tabla de abajo. Luego, pídale que conteste las preguntas para determinar si se está alimentando adecuadamente.

Mis alimentos de hoy

Desayuno	
Almuerzo	
Cena	
Refrigerios	

Preguntas

1. ¿Cuáles frutas y vegetales comiste hoy?

2. ¿Tomaste leche baja en grasa o yogurt, o comiste queso?

3. ¿Comiste pan, un cereal, arroz o pasta?

4. ¿Comiste carne, pescado, frijoles, huevos o nueces?

© Harcourt

School-Home Connection

A Note to Family Members

What We Are Learning About Health

In Chapter 4 of *Harcourt Health and Fitness*, we are learning about

- staying fit and keeping the body safe during physical activities.
- the importance of sleep in maintaining overall body health.
- avoiding injury by making responsible decisions about safety.
- being fair to others by following the rules of a game or sport.

Visit **www.harcourtschool.com/health** for links to parent resources.

How You Can Help

Parental involvement in the school environment is part of a coordinated school health plan that includes the home, school, community, and social services. You can support your school through increased communication and by volunteering your time or talents. At home you can support your child's learning by

- encouraging your child to find exercise that he or she likes.
- praising your child when he or she shows responsibility for personal safety.
- reviewing the rules of your child's favorite game or sport.

A Family Activity

Have your child help plan family exercise time. First, survey family members for their exercise preferences. Help your child fill out the table. Then, use the information to come up with an exercise activity in which the whole family can participate.

Your Family's Exercise

Family Member	Favorite Kind of Exercise	Best Time to Exercise

La escuela y la casa

Nota para los familiares

Lo que estamos aprendiendo acerca de la Salud

En el Capítulo 4 de *Harcourt Health and Fitness* estamos aprendiendo acerca de:

- Cómo hacer ejercicio sin lesionarse y cómo mantener un buen estado físico.
- La importancia de dormir el tiempo adecuado para la salud.
- Cómo tomar decisiones correctas al hacer ejercicio para evitar lesiones.
- La importancia de obedecer las reglas en los juegos y respetar a los otros jugadores.

 Visite **www.harcourtschool.com/health** para encontrar enlaces con recursos en inglés para los padres.

Cómo puede usted ayudar

La participación familiar en las actividades escolares forma parte de un plan de salud organizado que incluye la casa, la escuela, la comunidad y los servicios sociales. Usted puede apoyar a la escuela manteniendo una buena comunicación y ofreciendo su tiempo y sus talentos como voluntario. En casa, usted puede apoyar el aprendizaje de su hijo(a) haciendo lo siguiente:

- Anímelo a participar más en las actividades físicas que le gusten.
- Elógielo cuando se responsabiliza por su seguridad.
- Examinen las reglas de uno de sus juegos o deportes favoritos.

Actividad familiar

Anime a su hijo(a) a planificar un tiempo de ejercicio familiar. Para ello, pídale que pregunte a todos en la familia cuáles ejercicios prefieren hacer y a qué hora del día, y escriba la información que recoja en la tabla. Luego, anímelo a crear una actividad de gimnasia en la que todos puedan participar.

Gimnasia en familia

Nombre del familiar	Ejercicio predilecto	Hora del día

© Harcourt

School-Home Connection

A Note to Family Members

What We Are Learning About Health

In Chapter 5 of *Harcourt Health and Fitness,* we are learning about

- staying safe at school and on the bus or in a car.
- wearing the correct safety gear when skating, biking, skateboarding, or riding a scooter.
- staying safe around strangers, bullies, and potentially violent situations.
- resolving conflicts with friends in a reasonable manner.

 Visit **www.harcourtschool.com/health** for links to parent resources.

How You Can Help

Parental involvement in the school environment is part of a coordinated school health plan that includes the home, school, community, and social services. You can support your school through increased communication and by volunteering your time or talents. At home you can support your child's learning by

- reviewing the safety rules for riding in a car.

- discussing how violence might start and ways to prevent it.

- role-playing how your child would resolve a conflict with his or her friends.

A Family Activity

Outside the home there are many things that are hazardous and can cause injuries. Help your child list the things he or she can do to stay safe outside. Encourage your child to come up with additional outside activities that require safety measures.

Road Safety

Activity	Things to Do to Stay Safe
Walking	
Skating	
Skateboarding	
Riding a bike	
Riding in a car or bus	

© Harcourt

La escuela y la casa

Nota para los familiares

Lo que estamos aprendiendo acerca de la Salud

En el Capítulo 5 de *Harcourt Health and Fitness* estamos aprendiendo acerca de:

- Las reglas de seguridad en la escuela, el autobús y el carro.
- La importancia de usar la protección adecuada al patinar y montar en bicicleta, monopatín o patineta.
- Cómo mantenerse seguro en presencia de extraños y bravucones, así como en circunstancias potencialmente violentas.
- Cómo resolver adecuadamente los conflictos entre amigos.

 Visite **www.harcourtschool.com/health** para encontrar enlaces con recursos en inglés para los padres.

Cómo puede usted ayudar

La participación familiar en las actividades escolares forma parte de un plan de salud organizado que incluye la casa, la escuela, la comunidad y los servicios sociales. Usted puede apoyar a la escuela manteniendo una buena comunicación y ofreciendo su tiempo y sus talentos como voluntario. En casa, usted puede apoyar el aprendizaje de su hijo(a) haciendo lo siguiente:

- Repasen las reglas de seguridad en el carro.
- Hablen sobre las actividades que pueden desencadenar actos de violencia y las maneras de evitarlas.
- Improvisen situaciones en las que su hijo(a) tenga que resolver un conflicto con un amigo.

Actividad familiar

Al realizar cualquier actividad fuera de la casa, hay que obedecer ciertas reglas para prevenir accidentes. Ayude a su hijo(a) a escribir las cosas que puede hacer para evitar lesionarse cada vez que participe en una de las actividades mencionadas en la tabla, y pídale que agregue otras actividades a la lista.

Mi seguridad fuera de la casa

Actividad	Lo que debo hacer para evitar lesiones
Caminar	
Patinar	
Andar en monopatín	
Montar en bicicleta	
Montar en carro o en autobús	

Name _____ Date _____

School-Home Connection

What We Are Learning About Health

In Chapter 6 of *Harcourt Health and Fitness*, we are learning about

- safety rules for dealing with fire and poisons in the home.
- safety around electricity and in the kitchen, using simple first aid to treat minor medical needs.
- communicating the correct information during an emergency.
- obeying laws, rules, and signs on the street, at school, and around water.

 Visit **www.harcourtschool.com/health** for links to parent resources.

How You Can Help

Parental involvement in the school environment is part of a coordinated school health plan that includes the home, school, community, and social services. You can support your school through increased communication and by volunteering your time or talents. At home you can support your child's learning by

- reviewing fire safety rules for your home.
- making clear what your child may and may not do in the kitchen.
- discussing why there are safety laws and rules in your neighborhood.

A Family Activity

Home hazards are major causes of injury. Work with your child to survey your home for hazards. Help your child record any you find. Talk about the hazards that can be easily remedied, such as toys on stairs or dangerous items within the reach of small children.

Hazards in Your Home

Fire and Electrical Hazards	Poison Hazards	Other Hazards

© Harcourt

La escuela y la casa

Lo que estamos aprendiendo acerca de la Salud

En el Capítulo 6 de *Harcourt Health and Fitness* estamos aprendiendo acerca de:

• Las reglas de seguridad para evitar incendios e intoxicaciones en el hogar.
• La seguridad en la cocina y con el uso de electrodomésticos, y los primeros auxilios para el tratamiento de lesiones menores.
• La importancia de la buena comunicación durante una emergencia.
• La importancia de obedecer las leyes, los reglamentos y las señales de tránsito en la calle, la escuela y lugares cerca del agua.

 Visite **www.harcourtschool.com/health** para encontrar enlaces con recursos en inglés para los padres.

Cómo puede usted ayudar

La participación familiar en las actividades escolares forma parte de un plan de salud organizado que incluye la casa, la escuela, la comunidad y los servicios sociales. Usted puede apoyar a la escuela manteniendo una buena comunicación y ofreciendo su tiempo y sus talentos como voluntario. En casa, usted puede apoyar el aprendizaje de su hijo(a) haciendo lo siguiente:

• Repasen las reglas de seguridad en el hogar.
• Recuérdele lo que puede y no puede hacer en la cocina.
• Hablen sobre las reglas de seguridad y las leyes que existen en su barrio.

Actividad familiar

Ayude a su hijo(a) a buscar las cosas que pueden resultar peligrosas y causar accidentes en su casa, y pídale que las escriba en la tabla de abajo. Algunas de estas cosas son fácilmente identificables, como juguetes pequeños y escaleras donde hay niños pequeños. Hablen de los cambios que pueden hacer para evitar que alguien se lesione.

Peligros en la casa

Cosas que podrían causar incendios	Cosas que podrían causar envenenamiento	Otros peligros

Name _____ Date _____

School-Home Connection

A Note to Family Members

What We Are Learning About Health

In Chapter 7 of *Harcourt Health and Fitness,* we are learning about

- the symptoms of common illnesses and ways to prevent the spread of pathogens that might cause illnesses.
- positive health behaviors that reduce the risk of disease.
- how stress can hinder the body's ability to defend against disease and ways to manage that stress.
- being a caring friend, helping out in times of need.

 Visit **www.harcourtschool.com/health** for links to parent resources.

How You Can Help

Parental involvement in the school environment is part of a coordinated school health plan that includes the home, school, community, and social services. You can support your school through increased communication and by volunteering your time or talents. At home you can support your child's learning by

- discussing what was done when a family member was ill.
- discussing ways to deal with stress.
- praising your child when he or she helps someone who is in need.

A Family Activity

Good health is affected by many factors, including exercise, rest, and a healthful diet. Have your child ask family members to identify one strategy the family member pursues or would like to pursue to stay healthy. Discuss the survey with your child. Ask your child how he or she might help a family member make a commitment to staying healthy.

Family Wellness Survey

Family Member	Wellness Strategy

La escuela y la casa

Lo que estamos aprendiendo acerca de la Salud

En el Capítulo 7 de *Harcourt Health and Fitness* estamos aprendiendo acerca de:

- Los síntomas de las enfermedades comunes y algunas maneras de prevenir la propagación de agentes patógenos que pueden causar enfermedades.
- Algunos comportamientos de salud positivos que reducen el riesgo de enfermedades.
- Cómo el estrés dificulta la habilidad del cuerpo para defenderse de enfermedades y algunas maneras de manejar este estrés.
- Cómo ser un buen amigo al ayudar a las personas cuando lo necesitan.

Cómo puede usted ayudar

La participación familiar en las actividades escolares forma parte de un plan de salud organizado que incluye la casa, la escuela, la comunidad y los servicios sociales. Usted puede apoyar a la escuela manteniendo una buena comunicación y ofreciendo su tiempo y sus talentos como voluntario. En casa, usted puede apoyar el aprendizaje de su hijo(a) haciendo lo siguiente:

- Hablen acerca de las medidas que se tomaron cuando un familiar estuvo enfermo.
- Comenten sobre algunas maneras de manejar el estrés.
- Elógielo cuando ayuda a una persona que lo necesita.

 Visite **www.harcourtschool.com/health** para encontrar enlaces con recursos en inglés para los padres.

Actividad familiar

Para lograr tener una buena salud, hay muchos factores que influyen como el ejercicio, el descanso y una dieta alimenticia balanceada. Pida a su hijo(a) que haga una encuesta entre los familiares para identificar una estrategia que practiquen o que quieran establecer para mantenerse saludables. Comenten los resultados de la encuesta. Pregúntele cómo ayudaría a un familiar que se quiere comprometer a practicar buenos hábitos para mantenerse saludable.

Bienestar familiar

Nombre del familiar	Estrategia

School-Home Connection

A Note to Family Members

What We Are Learning About Health

In Chapter 8 of *Harcourt Health and Fitness,* we are learning about

- how drugs may be helpful or harmful.
- prescription and over-the-counter drugs and how they help people who are ill.
- illegal drugs and how they are harmful to those who take them.
- refusing to be put into dangerous situations.

 Visit **www.harcourtschool.com/health** for links to parent resources.

How You Can Help

Parental involvement in the school environment is part of a coordinated school health plan that includes the home, school, community, and social services. You can support your school through increased communication and by volunteering your time or talents. At home you can support your child's learning by

- discussing the kinds of prescription or over-the-counter medicines you have taken in the past.
- practicing ways to refuse illegal drugs.
- praising your child when he or she refuses to be put into dangerous situations by peers.

A Family Activity

Locate two prescription medicines and two over-the-counter medicines. Show these medicines to your child and then work with your child to complete the following table. In the first column, write the name of the medicine. In the second column, write whether the medicine is prescription or over-the-counter. When the table is completed, discuss with your child how he or she can tell the difference between over-the-counter medicines and prescription medicines.

Medicines in Your Home

Name of Medicine	Prescription or Over-the-Counter

© Harcourt

La escuela y la casa

Lo que estamos aprendiendo acerca de la Salud

En el Capítulo 8 de *Harcourt Health and Fitness* estamos aprendiendo acerca de:

• Cómo los medicamentos pueden ser eficaces o perjudiciales para la salud.

• Los medicamentos que requieren receta médica y los que no requieren receta médica y cómo ayudan a las personas que están enfermas.

• Las drogas ilegales y los daños que causan a las personas que las toman.

• Cómo negarse a participar en actividades que lleven a situaciones peligrosas.

 Visite **www.harcourtschool.com/health** para encontrar enlaces con recursos en inglés para los padres.

Cómo puede usted ayudar

La participación familiar en las actividades escolares forma parte de un plan de salud organizado que incluye la casa, la escuela, la comunidad y los servicios sociales. Usted puede apoyar a la escuela manteniendo una buena comunicación y ofreciendo su tiempo y sus talentos como voluntario. En casa, usted puede apoyar el aprendizaje de su hijo(a) haciendo lo siguiente:

• Hablen acerca de todos los medicamentos que hayan tomado en el pasado.

• Pongan en práctica diversas maneras de rechazar drogas ilegales.

• Elógielo cuando se niega a participar con sus amigos en actividades que lo lleven a situaciones peligrosas.

Actividad familiar

Consiga dos medicamentos que requieran receta médica y dos que no requieran receta médica. Muéstreselos a su hijo(a) y luego ayúdelo a completar la siguiente tabla. En la primera columna, escriba el nombre del medicamento. En la segunda columna, escriba si para conseguirlo se requiere una receta médica o no. Cuando terminen la tabla, comenten acerca de las diferencias entre ambas clases de medicamentos.

Los medicamentos en el hogar

Nombre del medicamento	Con receta médica/ Sin receta médica

School-Home Connection

A Note to Family Members

What We Are Learning About Health

In Chapter 9 of *Harcourt Health and Fitness,* we are learning about

- the different forms of tobacco and their adverse health effects.
- the immediate and long-term effects alcohol has on people.
- refusing peer pressure to use alcohol or tobacco.
- being trustworthy and following family rules.

 Visit **www.harcourtschool.com/health** for links to parent resources.

How You Can Help

Parental involvement in the school environment is part of a coordinated school health plan that includes the home, school, community, and social services. You can support your school through increased communication and by volunteering your time or talents. At home you can support your child's learning by

- examining the use of alcohol and tobacco in your community.
- role-playing ways to refuse alcohol and tobacco.
- praising your child for following rules when you are not around.

A Family Activity

Each day people are exposed to advertisements promoting alcohol. These advertisements appear in newspapers and magazines and on billboards and television. Have your child find an example of one of these advertisements. Discuss the advertisement with your child. What message is the advertiser trying to convey about the product? What does your child know about the product that might discredit this claim? Help your child record the results of your discussion in a table like the one below.

Alcohol Advertisement
Product name:
What the advertiser claims about the product:
What I know is true about the product:

La escuela y la casa

Lo que estamos aprendiendo acerca de la Salud

En el Capítulo 9 de *Harcourt Health and Fitness* estamos aprendiendo acerca de:

- Las diferentes formas de tabaco y sus efectos nocivos en la salud.
- Los efectos nocivos del alcohol a largo y corto plazo en la salud de las personas.
- Cómo resistir la influencia negativa que pueden ejercer algunos compañeros para usar alcohol o tabaco.
- Cómo ser una persona digna de confianza y seguir las reglas del hogar.

 Visite **www.harcourtschool.com/health** para encontrar enlaces con recursos en inglés para los padres.

Cómo puede usted ayudar

La participación familiar en las actividades escolares forma parte de un plan de salud organizado que incluye la casa, la escuela, la comunidad y los servicios sociales. Usted puede apoyar a la escuela manteniendo una buena comunicación y ofreciendo su tiempo y sus talentos como voluntario. En casa, usted puede apoyar el aprendizaje de su hijo(a) haciendo lo siguiente:

- Revisen las reglas acerca del uso del alcohol y tabaco de su comunidad.
- Improvisen algunas maneras en las que su hijo(a) actúe rechazando el alcohol y el tabaco.
- Elógielo cuando sigue las reglas del hogar, sin necesidad de que lo estén vigilando.

Actividad familiar

Cada día las personas están expuestas a los avisos publicitarios que promueven el uso del alcohol. Estos avisos se presentan en televisión, vallas publicitarias, periódicos y revistas. Pida a su hijo(a) que busque un ejemplo de uno de estos avisos. Juntos, analicen el aviso. ¿Qué mensaje está tratando de transmitir el anunciante acerca del producto? ¿Qué sabe su hijo(a) acerca del producto que desacreditaría este aviso? Ayúdelo a anotar las respuestas en una tabla parecida a la de abajo.

Aviso publicitario sobre el alcohol
Nombre del producto:
Lo que el anunciante dice acerca del producto:
Lo que sé que es cierto acerca del producto:

School-Home Connection

A Note to Family Members

What We Are Learning About Health

In Chapter 10 of *Harcourt Health and Fitness,* we are learning about

- where feelings come from and how to express those feelings in appropriate ways.
- ways to build positive relationships with family and friends.
- managing stress in healthful ways, such as reading or listening to music.
- being a good friend by caring, respecting differences, and being a good listener.

 Visit **www.harcourtschool.com/health** for links to parent resources.

How You Can Help

Parental involvement in the school environment is part of a coordinated school health plan that includes the home, school, community, and social services. You can support your school through increased communication and by volunteering your time or talents. At home you can support your child's learning by

- encouraging your child's positive friendships and relationships.
- coming up with ways to deal with stress in everyday situations.
- practicing listening skills, which are part of being a good friend.

A Family Activity

With your child, make a collage of feelings. Begin by collecting old newspapers and magazines. Then ask your child to find pictures of people whose expressions or body language reflect particular feelings, such as happiness, sadness, anger, or love. Work with your child to cut out the pictures and mount them on a large sheet of paper or poster board. Under each picture, have your child label the feeling or emotion. Discuss how your child shows these and other emotions.

© Harcourt

La escuela y la casa

Nota para los familiares

Lo que estamos aprendiendo acerca de la Salud

En el Capítulo 10 de *Harcourt Health and Fitness* estamos aprendiendo acerca de:

- Los sentimientos y cómo expresarlos apropiadamente.
- Algunas maneras de establecer relaciones positivas con la familia y amigos.
- Algunas maneras saludables para manejar el estrés como leyendo o escuchando música.
- Cómo ser un buen amigo al pensar en los demás, respetar las diferencias entre las personas y escuchar con atención.

 Visite **www.harcourtschool.com/health** para encontrar enlaces con recursos en inglés para los padres.

Cómo puede usted ayudar

La participación familiar en las actividades escolares forma parte de un plan de salud organizado que incluye la casa, la escuela, la comunidad y los servicios sociales. Usted puede apoyar a la escuela manteniendo una buena comunicación y ofreciendo su tiempo y sus talentos como voluntario. En casa, usted puede apoyar el aprendizaje de su hijo(a) haciendo lo siguiente:

- Elogie las buenas amistades y relaciones de su hijo(a).
- Preséntele algunas ideas de cómo manejar el estrés de las situaciones que manejamos a diario.
- Practiquen cómo escuchar con atención a los demás para ser un buen amigo.

Actividad familiar

Junto con su niño, hagan un collage de sentimientos. Recopilen periódicos viejos y revistas. Luego, pídale que busque fotografías de personas que reflejen un sentimiento en particular como felicidad, tristeza, ira o amor. Corten y peguen las fotografías en una cartulina o en una hoja de papel grande. Debajo de cada fotografía, pídale que escriba el sentimiento o emoción que muestra la foto. Hablen acerca de cómo su hijo(a) expresa éstas y otras emociones.

© Harcourt

Name _____   Date _____

School-Home Connection

A Note to Family Members

What We Are Learning About Health

In Chapter 11 of *Harcourt Health and Fitness,* we are learning about

- understanding families, ways they communicate, and things that are important to them.
- ways families can change and dealing with that change appropriately.
- resolving family conflicts by listening to and understanding what others want.
- being fair and doing a fair share to avoid taking advantage of other family members.

 Visit **www.harcourtschool.com/health** for links to parent resources.

How You Can Help

Parental involvement in the school environment is part of a coordinated school health plan that includes the home, school, community, and social services. You can support your school through increased communication and by volunteering your time or talents. At home you can support your child's learning by

- examining some of your family values and rituals.
- discussing any changes your family has gone through and how they made your child feel.
- making a list of chores for each family member.

A Family Activity

Help your child identify at least three different types of families that exist in your neighborhood or community. Enter your findings in the following table. In the first column, identify the type of family, such as single-female-parent. In the second column, list the members of the family, such as a mother and son. Discuss the table with your child. How are the families alike? How are they different?

Types of Families in Your Community

Type of Family	Family Members

La escuela y la casa

Nota para los familiares

Lo que estamos aprendiendo acerca de la Salud

En el Capítulo 11 de *Harcourt Health and Fitness* estamos aprendiendo acerca de:

- Cómo entender a las familias, las maneras como se comunican y las cosas que son importantes para ellas.
- Algunas maneras como las familias cambian y cómo adaptarse a ese cambio.
- Cómo resolver las diferencias de opinión al saber escuchar y entender lo que otros quieren.
- Cómo ser justos y no aprovecharnos de otros familiares.

 Visite **www.harcourtschool.com/health** para encontrar enlaces con recursos en inglés para los padres.

Cómo puede usted ayudar

La participación familiar en las actividades escolares forma parte de un plan de salud organizado que incluye la casa, la escuela, la comunidad y los servicios sociales. Usted puede apoyar a la escuela manteniendo una buena comunicación y ofreciendo su tiempo y sus talentos como voluntario. En casa, usted puede apoyar el aprendizaje de su hijo(a) haciendo lo siguiente:

- Revisen algunos de los valores y normas de la familia.
- Comenten acerca de los cambios que han tenido en la familia y cómo éstos afectaron a su hijo(a).
- Hagan una lista de las tareas del hogar que cada familiar debe hacer.

Actividad familiar

Ayude a su hijo(a) a identificar por lo menos tres tipos de familia diferentes que vivan en su vecindario o comunidad. Escriban los resultados en la siguiente tabla. En la primera columna, identifiquen el tipo de familia, como madre soltera. En la segunda columna, hagan una lista de los familiares, como madre e hijo. Analicen la tabla. ¿En qué se parecen las familias? ¿En qué se diferencian?

Tipos de familia en su comunidad

Tipo de familia	Familiares

© Harcourt

School-Home Connection

A Note to Family Members

What We Are Learning About Health

In Chapter 12 of *Harcourt Health and Fitness,* we are learning about

- health-care services in the community and their roles in helping everyone.
- where pollution comes from and the effect it has on the community.
- setting goals to reduce pollution and trash.
- taking pride in one's school through various activities, such as having a good attitude or throwing trash away.

Visit **www.harcourtschool.com/health** for links to parent resources.

How You Can Help

Parental involvement in the school environment is part of a coordinated school health plan that includes the home, school, community, and social services. You can support your school through increased communication and by volunteering your time or talents. At home you can support your child's learning by

- reviewing different health-care services in your community.
- discussing sources of pollution in your own neighborhood or city.
- praising your child's efforts to help keep his or her school a clean and safe place.

A Family Activity

Help your child survey three or four family members or friends who have used, visited, or worked at a community hospital to find out about some of the services it offers. If possible, have your child interview people who represent a range of age groups. Work with your child to summarize his or her findings in the following table. A sample has been provided to get you started.

My Local Hospital

Who	What
Aunt Marsha	Joined a support group for new mothers

© Harcourt

La escuela y la casa

Nota para los familiares

Lo que estamos aprendiendo acerca de la Salud

En el Capítulo 12 de *Harcourt Health and Fitness* estamos aprendiendo acerca de:

• Los centros de salud de la comunidad y sus funciones para ayudar a las personas.
• La contaminación y los efectos que tiene en la comunidad.
• Cómo establecer algunas metas para reducir la contaminación y la basura.
• Cómo mostrar que estamos orgullosos de nuestra escuela al mantenerla limpia y tener una buena actitud.

 Visite **www.harcourtschool.com/health** para encontrar enlaces con recursos en inglés para los padres.

Cómo puede usted ayudar

La participación familiar en las actividades escolares forma parte de un plan de salud organizado que incluye la casa, la escuela, la comunidad y los servicios sociales. Usted puede apoyar a la escuela manteniendo una buena comunicación y ofreciendo su tiempo y sus talentos como voluntario. En casa, usted puede apoyar el aprendizaje de su hijo(a) haciendo lo siguiente:

• Analicen los diferentes centros de salud de su comunidad.
• Hablen acerca de las fuentes de contaminación de su vecindario o ciudad.
• Elogie los esfuerzos de su hijo(a) por ayudar a que su escuela se mantenga siempre limpia y sea un lugar seguro.

Actividad familiar

Ayude a su hijo(a) a entrevistar tres o cuatro familiares o amigos que hayan usado, visitado o trabajado en un hospital de la comunidad, con el fin de averiguar acerca de los servicios que ofrece. Si es posible, pídale que entreviste personas que representen a grupos de distintas edades. Ayúdele a resumir los resultados de la encuesta en la siguiente tabla, siguiendo el ejemplo.

El hospital de la comunidad

Quién	Qué
Mi tía Marsha	Participó en un grupo para ayudar a las mujeres que iban a ser madres por primera vez

© Harcourt

Writing Models

The writing models on the following pages are examples of writing for different purposes. Students can consult these models as they work on the writing assignments in the Lesson Summary and Reviews in *Harcourt Health and Fitness*. You may wish to distribute copies of the writing models for students to keep.

You will also find rubrics to use for scoring writing assignments. There are rubrics for Ideas/Content Organization, Sentence Fluency, Word Choice, Conventions, and Voice.

Write to Express

Write to Inform

Write to Entertain

© Harcourt

Model: Business Letter

In a **business letter**, the writer may request information or express an opinion. A business letter has the same parts as a friendly letter, plus an inside address. This is the receiver's address.

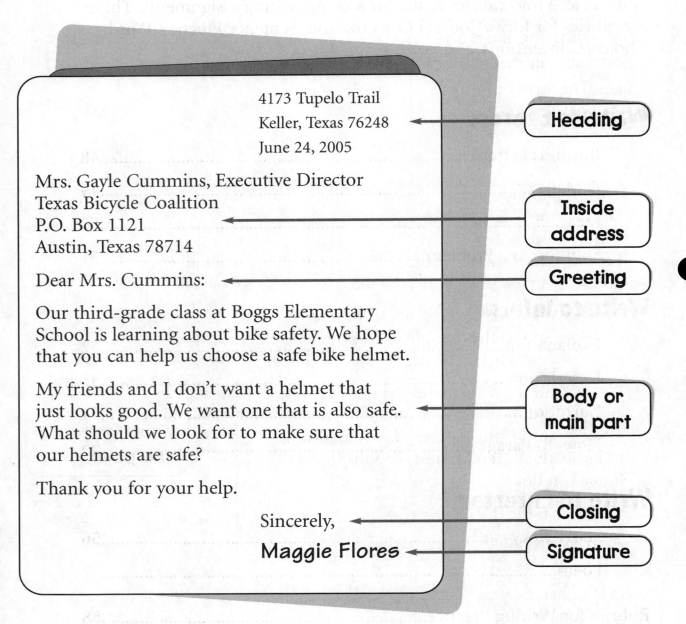

4173 Tupelo Trail
Keller, Texas 76248
June 24, 2005

Heading

Mrs. Gayle Cummins, Executive Director
Texas Bicycle Coalition
P.O. Box 1121
Austin, Texas 78714

Inside address

Dear Mrs. Cummins:

Greeting

Our third-grade class at Boggs Elementary School is learning about bike safety. We hope that you can help us choose a safe bike helmet.

My friends and I don't want a helmet that just looks good. We want one that is also safe. What should we look for to make sure that our helmets are safe?

Body or main part

Thank you for your help.

Sincerely,

Closing

Maggie Flores

Signature

© Harcourt

Model: E-Mail

Sending **e-mail** is like sending a letter. However, it should be short and to the point. You may wish to include a greeting and a signature. Include a subject line to describe your e-mail.

> Tell what the message is about on the subject line. The computer will put in the date.

Subj: Nursing Career
Date: September 25, 2005
From: Smartkid@abc.com
To: Nurse@university.com

In school, we are learning about different careers. I am in third grade. I would like to be a nurse when I grow up.

Please send me information about becoming a nurse. I want to know how many years of school a nurse must attend. I would also like to know the different kinds of jobs that a nurse can do.

Thank you for the information.

Ann Smith

> Be careful when you type in the e-mail address.

> Be sure your message is short and to the point.

© Harcourt

Writing in Health

Model: Idea

An **idea** is a thought about something you would like to make or do. Choose an idea you had, and tell how that idea came into your mind. Write the steps that were needed to carry out your idea. Tell whether your idea was a success.

Prepared to Escape

A firefighter came to our class and told us what to do in case of a fire. "Always drop down and stay low. This keeps you below the smoke," said the firefighter. "Crawl out quickly. Shout to warn others in your family about the fire."

The firefighter also told us to talk with family members about escape paths and a meeting place. This gave me a great idea.

> What was your idea? How did you think of it?

That night I told my family what I had learned in school that day. We decided on an escape plan for each of us and a meeting place. "I'm going to surprise you with a fire drill," I said proudly.

One evening after dinner, I grabbed the dinner bell and started ringing it loudly, shouting, "Fire drill! Fire drill!"

> What steps did you take to carry out your idea?

I made sure that everyone in the family heard the bell. Then I walked quickly over to our neighbor's house, which was the family meeting place. All my family members made it to the meeting place in less than a minute. Even the dog was there!

I could not wait to write a letter to the firefighter to tell him that I had planned and carried out a fire drill with my family. The drill was a great success. If we ever have a fire, we will know just what to do to stay safe.

> Did your idea prove to be a good one? How did you feel in the end?

© Harcourt

Writing in Health

Model: Solution to a Problem

You develop a **solution to a problem** by thinking of ways to solve the problem. Choose a problem you had. Explain what might have happened if you had not chosen the solution you did. Then describe the solution you chose, and tell if it was a good choice.

A Dangerous Brain

John was new to my neighborhood. He had just moved here from another state, and his house was two houses down from mine. I was happy to have the "new kid" live near me—that is, until I found out that he had dangerous ideas.

After school one day, John and I decided to go to the model store in the mall. I had just gotten some money for my birthday and was ready to spend it.

I saw John looking at the glue. "Do you need some for your model airplanes?" I asked.

"No," John said and started sniffing the glue. "Try it. It will make you feel really weird."

I was afraid, because I had never been around someone who did something so dangerous. I didn't know what to do at first. I knew that John would laugh at me if I didn't try it. More importantly, though, I knew that sniffing something like that could damage my brain.

"I have only one brain, John," I said, "and I don't want to hurt it." I started to walk away.

"Come on!" John said. "Trust me."

"No. I want to find an airplane model," I said. "I don't want to be anywhere near something so dangerous!"

I went to buy my model, but John didn't come with me.

I walked home by myself that day, and I didn't do things with John after that. I just didn't want to be with someone who made such dangerous choices.

> **What was the problem?**

> **What could have happened if you had not chosen that solution?**

> **Was your solution a good choice?**

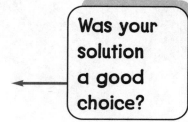

© Harcourt

Writing in Health

Model: Explanation

In an **explanation**, the writer helps the reader understand something. Use exact words to explain what something is, how something works, what happens during a process, or why something happens. Do not include your personal viewpoint in an explanation.

What Good Is Earwax?

You may wonder why you have wax in your ears. Also, you may think that earwax makes your ears dirty. The fact is that earwax is in your ears to help keep them clean.

> Include a topic sentence.

Think about all the tiny particles of dust and dirt that are in the air. Dust, dirt, and germs are always in the air. They could easily get deep inside your ear if your ear did not have earwax. Instead, the particles stick to the earwax, so the inside of your ear stays clean.

> Give a detailed explanation.

When you wash your ears, you should wash in, around, and behind your outer ear. You may be tempted to put a cotton-tipped stick into your ear canal to clean it or to scratch an itch. However, you should not do this, because you could damage your ear canal. Also, do not try to dig the earwax out of your ear. The old wax will work its way to your outer ear as you move your mouth to chew or talk. The inside of your ear cleans itself.

> Use exact words.

The next time you feel wax in your ears, think of it as a vacuum cleaner for the ears.

© Harcourt

Writing in Health

Model: Description

A **description** tells about an object, a place, a feeling, or something else the writer would like to describe. Use vivid words to tell what things look, feel, taste, smell, and sound like. You may also tell readers how you feel by giving your personal viewpoint.

Dinnertime at My House

I opened the door and knew that dinner was almost ready. Momma told me that I was late as I heard the screen door slam behind me. I could feel the sweat dripping down my face. I had run all the way home.

The smell of lasagna was in the air as Sheila pulled it from the oven. She helps Momma with dinner every night. Brent was placing napkins at each plate. I knew that it was time for me to pour the milk into the glasses. I could hear my stomach growl. I tore off a crust of warm bread as I passed by the bread basket. Momma's store sells the best bread in town.

The dog was barking loudly. That reminded me of my next job. I walked to the mudroom and reached for Skipper's water bowl. I filled it with water, and then I tipped the huge bag of dog food toward his food bowl. I could hear the clinking of the chunks of food as they hit the stainless steel. Skipper started to crunch his food. That would keep him busy while the rest of us ate. Momma smiled at me, proud that she didn't have to remind me to feed the dog.

The doorknob turned, and Daddy came in. He hung his coat in the closet. We all sat down, ready to have another delicious meal. Brent talked about his football game. Then Momma told a story about a lady who had come into the store that day. We all laughed. I had a story to tell about why I was late. Dinnertime is the best part of the day for my family.

> Describe your **topic** in a main idea sentence.

> Use **vivid words** in the detail sentences.

> Express your personal viewpoint.

© Harcourt

Writing in Health

Model: Personal Narrative

A **personal narrative** is a story about the writer's own experiences. The writer often tells about a lesson he or she learned or a significant event that helped him or her understand something differently.

A Penny Saved

Like most third graders, I do not have a lot of money. Mom gave me five dollars to buy treats for my slumber party. I went right to work finding out how to get the most for my money.

> **Introduce yourself.**

Mom said that she wanted me to check the food labels when I shopped. She did not want me to serve my friends a snack that had an unhealthful ingredient listed on its label. I had a lot of work to do.

Most of the snack foods that were at the top of my list were advertised on television. Mom said that those ads had cost the snack-food companies a lot of money. She was right. Each one of the snacks in the ads was more expensive than the store brand. I crossed those snacks off my list.

> **Describe the event that caused you to change.**

Some of the snack foods with labels that said "low in fat" were high in sugar. Mom did not want my friends and me to eat too much sugar. I crossed those foods off my list, too.

I thought about buying drink boxes for my friends. I quickly found out that those fancy boxes were not cheap. This was harder than I had thought it would be.

> **Tell how the event changed you.**

What did I end up buying my slumber party guests for yummy treats? I got the store-brand bag of pretzels and a large container of juice that we could share. At home I found some cartoon cups and straws to use. Mom was proud of me for having ninety-eight cents left when I was finished!

© Harcourt

Writing Model

Model: How-To Paragraph

In a **how-to paragraph**, the writer gives steps to tell how to make or do something. List all the materials the reader will need for the activity. Tell the steps in the right order.

Brushing and Flossing

It isn't enough to just brush your teeth. To remove plaque from between your teeth, you must use dental floss. You will need a piece of dental floss about 18 inches long. You will use the same piece of floss on all your teeth. First, wrap one end of the floss around the middle finger of one hand. Next, use your thumbs and index fingers to guide the floss, pulling it gently between two teeth. It is important to move the floss all the way to the gum line of the teeth. If the floss gets stuck between your teeth, pull it straight out and try again. Then, remove the floss, and unwind it a bit to reach a clean part. Finally, begin flossing the next space between two teeth, and continue until all the spaces have been flossed.

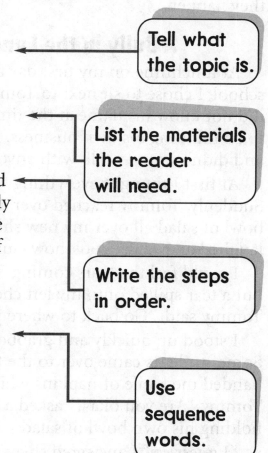

Tell what the topic is.

List the materials the reader will need.

Write the steps in order.

Use sequence words.

© Harcourt

Writing in Health

Model: Story

A **story** includes characters, a setting, and a plot. The characters in a story can be real or imaginary. The main character in a story has a problem to solve. Tell the events of the story in the order in which they happen.

A Bully in the Lunchroom

At lunchtime on my first day at my new school, I chose to sit next to Tommy Greeber. I did not know his name at the time, but he seemed to be minding his own business. I was nervous and didn't want to talk with anyone.

At first I thought everything would be all right. Suddenly, Tommy reached over and dumped my bowl of salad all over my new shirt. Then he laughed and said, "Look how clumsy you are!"

I could feel the tears coming. I tried not to cry, but a tear spilled onto my left cheek. "Crybaby," Tommy said. "Go back to where you came from."

I stood up quickly and grabbed my backpack. Some students came over to the table. One handed me a pile of napkins while glaring at Tommy. "Are you okay?" asked a boy who was holding his own bowl of salad.

"I guess so," I answered shyly.

"Come over and sit with us," said a girl with a big smile. "Tommy can be a bully." Just then, my new teacher led Tommy out of the cafeteria.

In class that afternoon, our teacher talked with us about bullies. We acted out ways to get along with one another instead of bullying.

In physical education class we played a softball game. Tommy was on my team. He can really throw the ball. I guess we can be friends—as long as he doesn't touch my salad again!

> Use exact words to tell about the problem that the main character has to solve.

> Give the events of the story in time order.

© Harcourt

Model: Poem

A **poem** is a way for the writer to describe something. People who write poems choose their words carefully. They use vivid words to help the reader know what the subject looks, sounds, feels, smells, and tastes like. Some poems rhyme, but some do not. Many poems have a rhythm, or beat, that makes them fun to read.

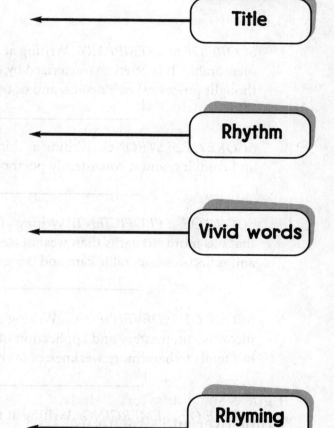

Rotten Eggs

This morning I had a nasty surprise
When I got some water to drink.
Someone had left a carton of eggs
On the counter next to the sink!
Left out overnight, they had surely
    spoiled,
And the germs inside had grown.
No scrambled eggs for breakfast
    today—
I left those eggs alone.
Throwing out food along with
    the trash
Could ruin anyone's day.
When you're finished with what
    you take from the fridge,
Please put the rest away!

Title

Rhythm

Vivid words

Rhyming words

Rubrics for Writing Practice

A Six-Point Scoring Scale

Student work produced for writing assessment can be scored by using a six-point scale. Although each rubric includes specific descriptors for each score point, each score can also be framed in a more global perspective.

SCORE OF 6: EXEMPLARY. Writing at this level is both exceptional and memorable. It is often characterized by distinctive and unusually sophisticated thought processes, rich details, and outstanding craftsmanship.

SCORE OF 5: STRONG. Writing at this level exceeds the standard. It is thorough and complex, and it consistently portrays exceptional control of content and skills.

SCORE OF 4: PROFICIENT. Writing at this level meets the standard. It is solid work that has more strengths than weaknesses. The writing demonstrates mastery of skills and reflects considerable care and commitment.

SCORE OF 3: DEVELOPING. Writing at this level shows basic, although sometimes inconsistent, mastery and application of content and skills. It shows some strengths but tends to have more weaknesses overall.

SCORE OF 2: EMERGING. Writing at this level is often superficial, fragmented, or incomplete. It may show a partial mastery of content and skills, but it needs considerable development before reflecting the proficient level of performance.

SCORE OF 1: BEGINNING. Writing at this level is minimal. It typically lacks understanding and use of appropriate skills and strategies. The writing may contain major errors.

Rubric for Ideas/Content

Score	Description
6	The writing is exceptionally clear, focused, and interesting. It holds the reader's attention throughout. Main ideas stand out and are developed by strong support and rich details suitable to the audience and the purpose.
5	The writing is clear, focused, and interesting. It holds the reader's attention. Main ideas stand out and are developed by supporting details suitable to the audience and the purpose.
4	The writing is clear and focused. The reader can easily understand the main ideas. Support is present, although it may be limited or rather general.
3	The reader can understand the main ideas, although they may be overly broad or simplistic, and the results may not be effective. Supporting details are often limited, insubstantial, overly general, or occasionally slightly off topic.
2	The main ideas and purpose are somewhat unclear, or development is attempted but minimal.
1	The writing lacks a central idea or purpose.

Rubric for Organization

Score	Description
6	The organization enhances the central idea(s) and its development. The order and structure are compelling and move the reader through the text easily.
5	The organization enhances the central idea(s) and its development. The order and structure are strong and move the reader through the text.
4	The organization is clear and coherent. Order and structure are present but may seem formulaic.
3	An attempt has been made to organize the writing; however, the overall structure is inconsistent or skeletal.
2	The writing lacks a clear organizational structure. An occasional organizational device is discernible; however, either the writing is difficult to follow and the reader has to reread substantial portions, or the piece is simply too short to demonstrate organizational skills.
1	The writing lacks coherence; organization seems haphazard and disjointed. Even after rereading, the reader remains confused.

© Harcourt

Rubric for Sentence Fluency

Score	Description
6	The writing has an effective flow and rhythm. Sentences show a high degree of craftsmanship, with consistently strong and varied structure that makes expressive oral reading easy and enjoyable.
5	The writing has an easy flow and rhythm. Sentences are carefully crafted, with strong and varied structure that makes expressive oral reading easy and enjoyable.
4	The writing flows; however, connections between phrases or sentences may be less than fluid. Sentence patterns are somewhat varied, contributing to ease in oral reading.
3	The writing tends to be mechanical rather than fluid. Occasional awkward constructions may force the reader to slow down or reread.
2	The writing tends to be either choppy or rambling. Awkward constructions often force the reader to slow down or reread.
1	The writing is difficult to follow or to read aloud. Sentences tend to be incomplete, rambling, or very awkward.

Rubric for Word Choice

Score	Description
6	The words convey the intended message in an exceptionally interesting, precise, and natural way appropriate to the audience and the purpose. The writer employs a rich, broad range of words that have been carefully chosen and thoughtfully placed for impact.
5	The words convey the intended message in an interesting, precise, and natural way appropriate to the audience and the purpose. The writer employs a broad range of words that have been carefully chosen and thoughtfully placed for impact.
4	The words effectively convey the intended message. The writer employs a variety of words that are functional and appropriate to the audience and the purpose.
3	The language is quite ordinary, lacking interest, precision, and variety, or may be inappropriate to the audience and the purpose in places. The writer does not employ a variety of words, producing a sort of "generic" paper filled with familiar words and phrases.
2	The language is monotonous and/or misused, detracting from the meaning and impact.
1	The writing shows an extremely limited vocabulary or is so filled with misuses of words that the meaning is obscured. Because of vague or imprecise language, only the most general kind of message is communicated.

© Harcourt

Rubric for Conventions

Score	Description
6	The writing demonstrates exceptionally strong control of standard writing conventions (e.g., punctuation, spelling, capitalization, paragraph breaks, grammar, and usage) and uses them effectively to enhance communication. Errors are so few and so minor that the reader can easily skim right over them unless specifically searching for them.
5	The writing demonstrates strong control of standard writing conventions (e.g., punctuation, spelling, capitalization, paragraph breaks, grammar, and usage) and uses them effectively to enhance communication. Errors are so few and so minor that they do not impede readability.
4	The writing demonstrates control of standard writing conventions (e.g., punctuation, spelling, capitalization, paragraph breaks, grammar, and usage). Minor errors, while perhaps noticeable, do not impede readability.
3	The writing demonstrates limited control of standard writing conventions (e.g., punctuation, spelling, capitalization, paragraph breaks, grammar, and usage). Errors begin to impede readability.
2	The writing demonstrates little control of standard writing conventions. Frequent, significant errors impede readability.
1	Numerous errors in usage, spelling, capitalization, and punctuation repeatedly distract the reader and make the text difficult to read. In fact, the severity and frequency of errors are so overwhelming that the reader finds it difficult to focus on the message and must reread for meaning.

Rubric for Voice

Score	Description
6	The writer has chosen a voice appropriate for the topic, purpose, and audience. The writer seems deeply committed to the topic, and there is an exceptional sense of "writing to be read." The writing is expressive, engaging, or sincere.
5	The writer has chosen a voice appropriate for the topic, purpose, and audience. The writer seems committed to the topic, and there is a sense of "writing to be read." The writing is expressive, engaging, or sincere.
4	A voice is present. The writer demonstrates commitment to the topic, and there may be a sense of "writing to be read." In places the writing is expressive, engaging, or sincere.
3	The writer's commitment to the topic seems inconsistent. A sense of the writer may emerge at times; however, the voice is either inappropriately personal or inappropriately impersonal.
2	The writing provides little sense of involvement or commitment. There is no evidence that the writer has chosen a suitable voice.
1	The writing seems to lack a sense of involvement or commitment.

© Harcourt

Identify Cause and Effect

Cause:

Effect:

Reading Skill Graphic Organizer

Compare and Contrast

Topic:

Alike

Different

Draw Conclusions

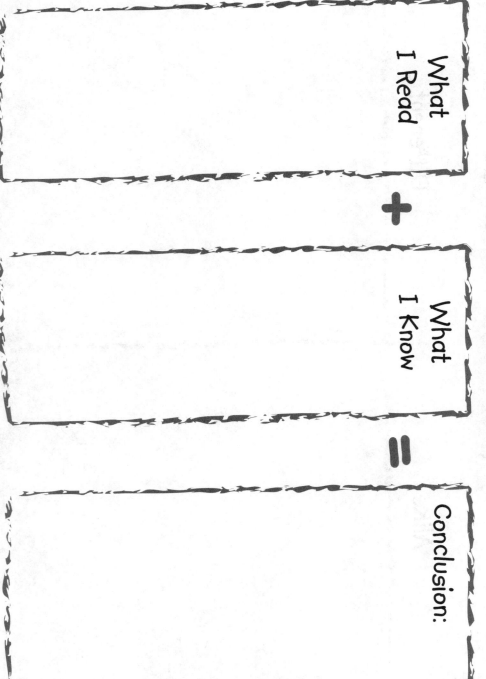

What I Read

+

What I Know

=

Conclusion:

Identify Main Idea and Details

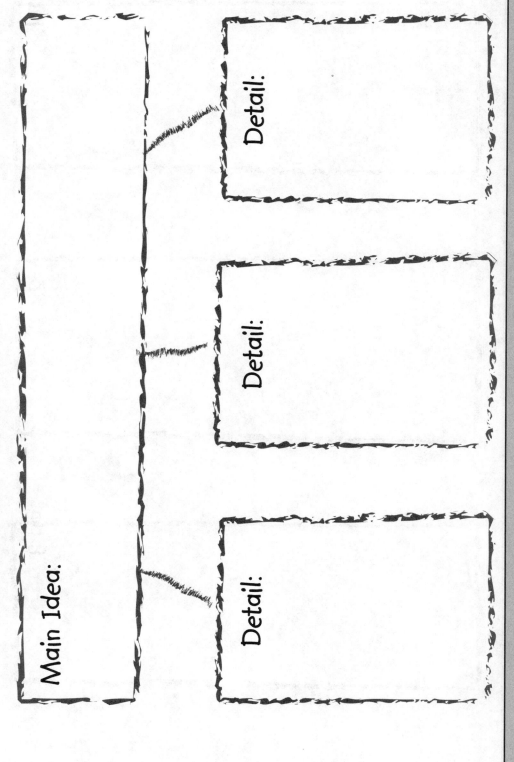

Main Idea:

Detail:

Detail:

Detail:

Reading Skill Graphic Organizer

Sequence

1.

2.

3.

Reading Skill Graphic Organizer

Focus Skill

Summarize

Summary:

=

Details:

+

Main Idea:

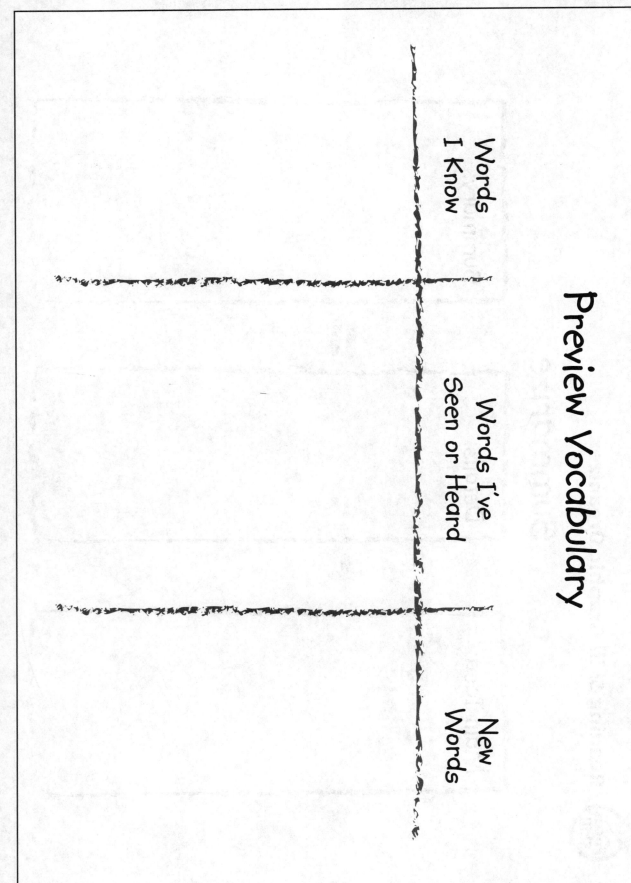

Preview Vocabulary

Words I Know

Words I've Seen or Heard

New Words

© Harcourt

Venn Diagram

K-W-L Chart

What I Know	What I Want to Know	What I Learned

Web

Chart

Knowledge Chart

Topic_____

Prior Knowledge	New Knowledge
1.	1.
2.	2.
3.	3.
4.	4.
5.	5.
6.	6.
7.	7.

Project Plan

What I Want to Find Out

1.

How I Can Find Out

2.

What I Need to Do

3.

Materials

How I Can Share Information

4.

Introduction to the Health and Safety Handbook

Using the Health and Safety Handbook

This section of Teaching Resources provides information that addresses important health concerns for students, such as nutrition, physical fitness, safety, and first aid. In addition, it identifies life skills and character traits that are learned early in life and are used in daily interaction with others. This section is intended to supplement and extend the content of the Student Edition.

In the Classroom

You can use these pages as stand-alone lessons. You may wish to make copies of these pages for students to compile in a personal health and safety handbook as you teach core lessons from the Student Edition.

At Home

You may wish to send copies of these pages home so that students can discuss the tips and topics with their families. The copies can also serve as a reference if students are completing health projects at home.

© Harcourt

Health and Safety Handbook
Contents

Understanding Life Skills

Having good health isn't just knowing the facts about what to eat or how to stay well. It's also thinking critically about those facts and knowing how to apply them to your daily life. Using life skills to apply your growing health knowledge can help you reach the goal of good health.

Communicate

In order to communicate well, you need to explain your ideas, needs, or feelings in a way that others can understand. You also need to listen to and try to understand what others have to say.

Steps for Communicating

1. Understand your audience.
2. Give a clear message.
3. Listen carefully, and answer any questions.
4. Gather feedback.

Ways to Give a Clear Message

- Use "I" messages.
- Use a respectful tone of voice.
- Make eye contact.
- Express ideas in a clear, organized way.

Make Responsible Decisions

When you make decisions, you think about a group of choices and decide on the wisest thing to do in order to avoid risky situations or health risks.

Steps for Making Responsible Decisions

1. Find out about the choices you could make.
2. Eliminate choices that are illegal or against your family rules.
3. Ask yourself: What is the possible result of each choice? Does the choice show good character?
4. Decide on what seems to be the best choice.

Understanding Life Skills

Manage Stress

Everyone feels stress. Knowing how to manage your stress can help you get through tense or exciting situations.

Steps for Managing Stress

1. Know what stress feels like and what causes it.

2. Try to determine the cause of the stress.

3. Do something that will help you relieve the feelings of stress.

Ways to Relieve Stress

- Take a walk, exercise, or play a sport.

- Talk to someone you trust about the way you're feeling.

- Watch a funny movie or television show.

Refuse

Knowing what to say *before* you are asked to do something you don't want to do can keep you moving toward good health.

How to Refuse

- Say **no** firmly, and state your reasons for saying **no**.

- Remember a consequence, and keep saying **no**.

- Suggest something else to do.

- Repeat **no**, and walk away. Leave the door open for the other person to join you.

Other Ways to Refuse

- Continue to repeat **no**.

- Change the subject.

- Avoid possible problem situations.

- Ignore the person. Give him or her the "cold shoulder."

© Harcourt

Understanding Life Skills

Resolve Conflicts

You must choose and use strategies to communicate and compromise in order to find solutions to problems or to avoid violence.

Steps for Resolving Conflicts

1. Use "I" messages to tell how you feel.

2. Listen to the other person. Consider the other person's point of view.

3. Talk about a solution.

4. Find a way for both sides to win.

Ways to Talk About a Solution

- Ask for a mediator.

- Walk away.

- Use humor.

Set Goals

When you set goals, you must decide on a change you want to make and then take actions to make that change happen.

Steps for Setting Goals

1. Choose a goal.

2. Plan steps to meet the goal. Determine whether you will need any help.

3. Check your progress as you work toward the goal.

4. Reflect on and evaluate your progress toward the goal.

Building Good Character

Caring	Citizenship	Fairness	Respect	Responsibility	Trustworthiness

These are values we choose to help guide us in our daily living. The rules that come from these values are the ground rules of good behavior.

Caring

"It is one of the most beautiful compensations of life, that no man can sincerely try to help another without helping himself."

—Ralph Waldo Emerson

DO
- Support and value family members.
- Be a good friend and share your feelings.
- Show concern for others.
- Thank people who help you.
- Help people in need.

DON'T
- Don't be selfish.
- Don't expect rewards for being caring.
- Don't gossip.
- Don't hurt anyone's feelings.

How do YOU show CARING?

Citizenship

"We must learn to live together as brothers or perish together as fools."

—Martin Luther King, Jr.

DO
- Take pride in your school, community, state, and country.
- Obey laws and rules and respect authority.
- Be a good neighbor.
- Help keep your school and neighborhood safe and clean.
- Cooperate with others.
- Protect the environment.

DON'T
- Don't break rules and laws.
- Don't waste natural resources.
- Don't damage public property or the property of others.
- Don't litter or hurt the environment in other ways.

How do YOU show CITIZENSHIP?

© Harcourt

Building Good Character

Caring	Citizenship	Fairness	Respect	Responsibility	Trustworthiness

These are values we choose to help guide us in our daily living. The rules that come from these values are the ground rules of good behavior.

Fairness

"Justice cannot be for one side alone, but must be for both."

—Eleanor Roosevelt

DO
- Play by the rules.
- Be a good sport.
- Share.
- Take turns.
- Listen to the opinions of others.

DON'T
- Don't take more than your share.
- Don't be a bad loser or a bad winner.
- Don't take advantage of others.
- Don't blame others without cause.
- Don't cut in front of others in line.

How do YOU show FAIRNESS?

Respect

"I believe . . . that every human mind feels pleasure in doing good to another."

—Thomas Jefferson

DO
- Treat others the way you want to be treated.
- Accept people who are different from you.
- Be polite and use good manners.
- Be considerate of the feelings of others.
- Stay calm when you are angry.
- Develop self-respect and self-confidence.

DON'T
- Don't use bad language.
- Don't insult or embarrass anyone.
- Don't threaten or bully anyone.
- Don't hit or hurt anyone.

How do YOU show RESPECT?

© Harcourt

Building Good Character

| Caring | Citizenship | Fairness | Respect | Responsibility | Trustworthiness |

These are values we choose to help guide us in our daily living. The rules that come from these values are the ground rules of good behavior.

Responsibility

"Responsibility is the price of greatness."

—Winston Churchill

DO
- Practice self-control.
- Express feelings, needs, and wants in appropriate ways.
- Practice good health habits.
- Keep yourself safe.
- Keep trying. Do your best.
- Complete tasks.
- Set goals and work toward them.
- Be a good role model.

DON'T
- Don't smoke. Don't use alcohol or other drugs.
- Don't do things that are unsafe or destructive.
- Don't be swayed by negative peer pressure.
- Don't deny or make excuses for your mistakes.
- Don't leave your work for others to do.
- Don't lose or misuse your belongings.

How do YOU show RESPONSIBILITY?

Trustworthiness

"What you do speaks so loudly that I cannot hear what you say."

—Ralph Waldo Emerson

DO
- Be honest. Tell the truth.
- Do the right thing.
- Report dangerous situations.
- Be dependable.
- Be loyal to your family, friends, and country.
- Take care of things you borrow, and return them promptly.

DON'T
- Don't tell lies.
- Don't cheat.
- Don't steal.
- Don't break promises.
- Don't borrow without asking first.

How do YOU show TRUSTWORTHINESS?

© Harcourt

Good Nutrition

MyPyramid

No one food or food group supplies everything your body needs for good health. That's why it's important to eat foods from all the food groups. MyPyramid can help you choose healthful foods in the right amounts. By choosing more foods from the groups with wide stripes and fewer foods from the group with narrow stripes, you will eat the foods that provide your body with energy to grow and develop.

The portions for each food group are suggested for children ages 6–10.

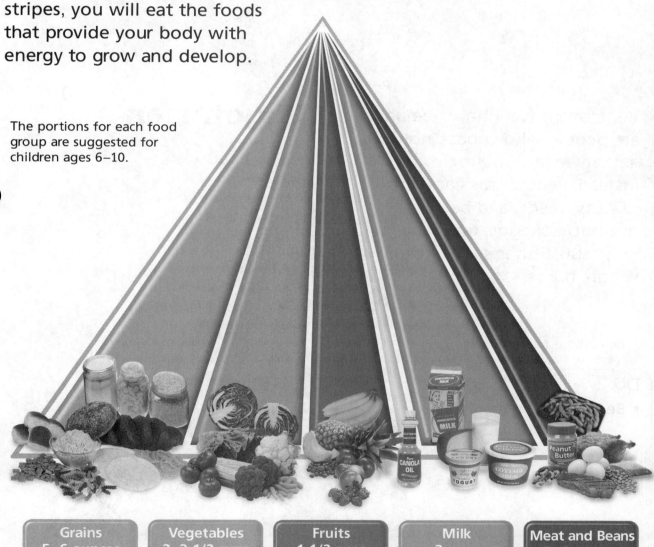

Grains	Vegetables	Fruits	Milk	Meat and Beans
5–6 ounces	2–2 1/2 cups	1 1/2 cups	3 cups	5–6 ounces

© Harcourt

Good Nutrition

More Food Guide Pyramids

MyPyramid from the U.S. Department of Agriculture (USDA) (page 83) shows common foods from the United States. Foods from different cultures and lifestyles also can make up a healthful diet. These other pyramids can help you add new foods to your diet. Use the portions guide on page 88 with all four pyramids.

Vegetarians (vej·uh·TAIR·ee·uhnz) are people who choose not to eat any meat, poultry, or fish. Instead, vegetarians eat a lot of nuts, seeds, and beans; nut butters; eggs; tofu; and meat substitutes such as veggie burgers.

The portions for each food group are suggested for children ages 9–13.

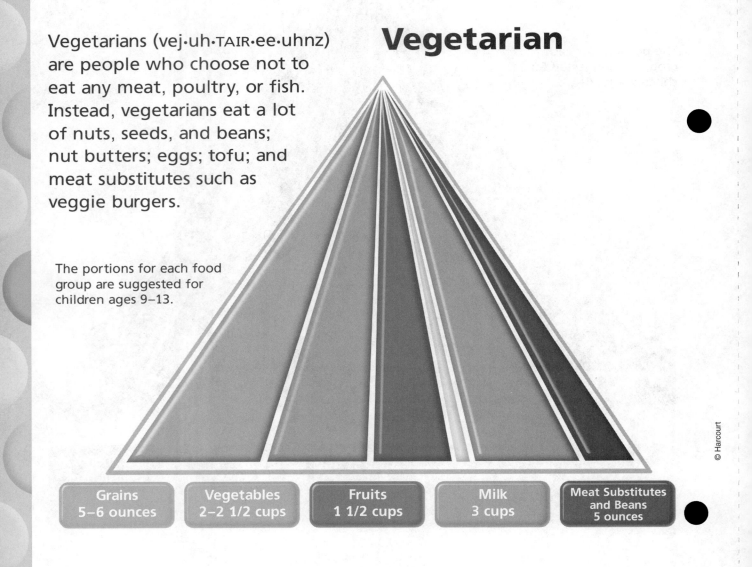

Vegetarian

| Grains 5–6 ounces | Vegetables 2–2 1/2 cups | Fruits 1 1/2 cups | Milk 3 cups | Meat Substitutes and Beans 5 ounces |

© Harcourt

These two pyramids organize foods differently from MyPyramid. You read these pyramids from the bottom up. Eat the foods at the bottom of the pyramid in greater amounts than those at the top. They also suggest eating seafood, poultry, eggs, and meat each week or month instead of each day. Moderate daily use of vegetable oils is also recommended.

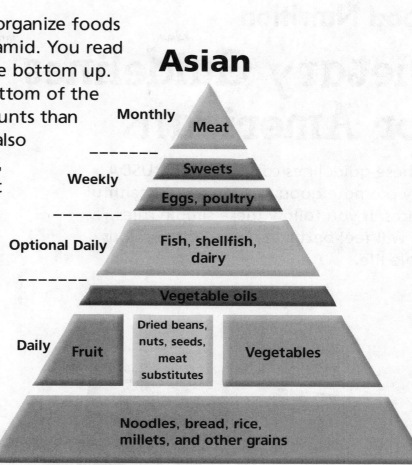

Asian

Monthly — Meat

Weekly — Sweets / Eggs, poultry

Optional Daily — Fish, shellfish, dairy

Vegetable oils

Daily — Fruit / Dried beans, nuts, seeds, meat substitutes / Vegetables

Noodles, bread, rice, millets, and other grains

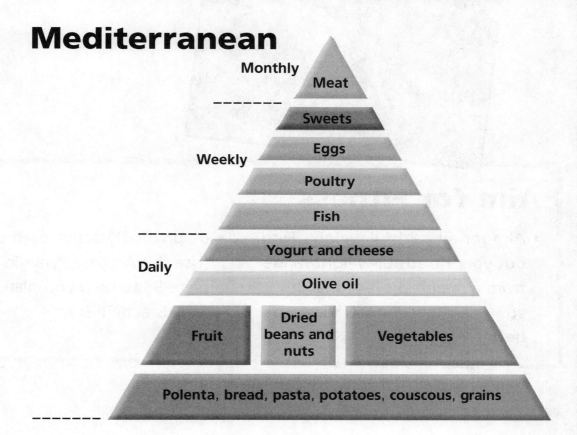

Mediterranean

Monthly — Meat

Sweets

Weekly — Eggs / Poultry / Fish

Yogurt and cheese

Daily — Olive oil

Fruit / Dried beans and nuts / Vegetables

Polenta, bread, pasta, potatoes, couscous, grains

© Harcourt

Good Nutrition

Dietary Guidelines for Americans

These guidelines come from the USDA. They promote good nutrition and healthful choices. If you follow these simple rules, you will feel better and be healthier your whole life.

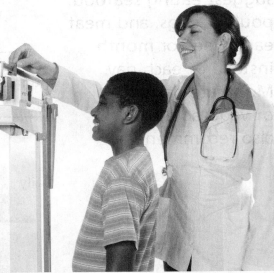

Aim for Fitness

- Aim for a healthful weight. Find out your healthful weight range from a health professional. If you need to, set goals to reach a better weight.

- Be physically active each day. (Use the Activity Pyramid on page 98 to help you plan each week's activities.)

© Harcourt

Build a Healthful Base

- Use a food guide pyramid to guide your food choices.

- Each day, choose a variety of grains, such as wheat, oats, rice, and corn. Choose whole grains when you can.

- Each day, choose a variety of fruits and vegetables.

- Keep food safe to eat. (Follow the tips on pages 89–90 for safely preparing and storing food.)

Choose Sensibly

- Choose a diet that is moderate in total fat and low in saturated fat and cholesterol.

- Choose foods and drinks that are low in sugar. Lower the amount of sugar you eat.

- Choose foods that are low in salt. When you prepare foods, use very little salt.

© Harcourt

Estimating Portions

Choosing a variety of foods is only half the story. You also need to choose the right portions. The table below can help you estimate how much you are eating of your favorite foods.

Estimating Serving Size

Food Group	Daily Portion	Easy Estimates
Grains	5–6 ounces	One ounce equals • one slice of bread • an ice cream scoop of cooked rice, oats, or pasta • a fistful of cereal flakes
Vegetables	2–$2\frac{1}{2}$ cups	One cup is about the size of • a baseball • a fist • two ice cream scoops
Fruits	$1\frac{1}{2}$ cups	A medium apple, pear, or orange equals about one cup.
Milk	3 cups	$1\frac{1}{2}$ ounces of cheese (about the size of three dominoes) provides about the same nutrients as one cup of milk.
Meat and Beans	5 ounces	One ounce of beans will fill an ice cream scoop. Three ounces of cooked meat, fish, or poultry is about the size of your palm or a computer mouse.

Oils should be eaten in small amounts—no more that 5 teaspoons per day. A teaspoon is about the size of a penny or a fingertip.

Fight Bacteria

You probably already know to throw away food that smells bad or looks moldy. But food doesn't have to look or smell bad to make you ill. To keep your food safe and yourself from becoming ill, follow the steps outlined in the picture below. And remember—when in doubt, throw it out!

FIGHT BAC!

Keep Food Safe From Bacteria ®

CLEAN
Wash hands and surfaces often.

SEPARATE
Don't cross-contaminate.

CHILL
Refrigerate promptly.

COOK
Cook to proper temperatures.

Preparing Foods Safely
Food Safety Tips
Tips for Preparing Food

- Wash hands in warm, soapy water before preparing food. It's also a good idea to wash hands after preparing each dish.

- Defrost meat in a microwave or the refrigerator.

- Keep raw meat, poultry, fish, and their juices away from other food.

- Wash cutting boards, knives, and countertops immediately after cutting up meat, poultry, or fish. Never use the same cutting board for meats and vegetables without washing the board first.

Tips for Cooking Food

- Cook all food completely, especially meat. Complete cooking kills the bacteria that can make you ill.

- Red meats should be cooked to a temperature of 160°F. Poultry should be cooked to 180°F. When done, fish flakes easily with a fork.

- Never eat food that contains raw eggs or raw egg yolks, including uncooked cookie dough.

Tips for Cleaning Up the Kitchen

- Wash all dishes, utensils, and countertops with hot, soapy water.

- Store leftovers in small containers that will cool quickly in the refrigerator. Don't leave leftovers on the counter to cool.

© Harcourt

Being Physically Active

Guidelines for a Good Workout

There are three things you should do every time you are going to exercise—warm up, work out, and cool down.

Warm Up When you warm up, your heartbeat rate, breathing rate, and body temperature increase and more blood flows to your muscles. As your body warms up, you can move more easily. People who warm up are less stiff after exercising, and are less likely to have exercise-related injuries. Your warm-up should include five minutes of stretching, and five minutes of low-level exercise. Some simple stretches are shown on pages 94–95.

Work Out The main part of your exercise routine should be an aerobic exercise that lasts twenty to thirty minutes. Aerobic exercises make your heart, lungs, and circulatory system stronger.

Some common aerobic exercises are shown on pages 92–93. You may want to mix up the types of activities you do. This helps you work different muscles and provides a better workout over time.

Cool Down When you finish your aerobic exercise, you need to give your body time to cool down. Start your cool-down with three to five minutes of low-level activity. End with stretching exercises to prevent soreness and stiffness.

Building a Strong Heart and Lungs

Aerobic activities cause deep breathing and a fast heartbeat rate for at least twenty minutes. These activities help both your heart and your lungs. Because your heart is a muscle, it gets stronger with exercise. A strong heart doesn't have to work as hard to pump blood to the rest of your body. Exercise also allows your lungs to hold more air. With a strong heart and lungs, your cells get oxygen faster and your body works more efficiently.

▲ **Swimming** Swimming is great for your endurance and flexibility. Even if you're not a great swimmer, you can use a kickboard and have a great time and a great workout just kicking around the pool. Be sure to swim only when a lifeguard is present.

◀ **In-line Skating** Remember to always wear a helmet when skating. Always wear protective pads on your elbows and knees, and guards on your wrists, too. Learning how to skate, stop, and fall correctly will make you a safer skater.

© Harcourt

Health and Safety Handbook

▲ Jumping Rope Jumping rope is one of the best ways to increase your endurance. Remember to always jump on an even surface and always wear supportive shoes.

▼ Walking A fast-paced walk is a terrific way to build your endurance. The only equipment you need is supportive shoes. Walking with a friend can make this exercise a lot of fun.

▼ Bicycling Bicycling provides good aerobic activity and a great way to see the outdoors. Be sure to learn and follow bicycle safety rules. And *always* remember to wear your helmet!

© Harcourt

Being Physically Active
Warm-Up and Cool-Down Stretches

Before you exercise, you should warm up your muscles. The warm-up exercises shown here should be held for at least fifteen to twenty seconds and repeated at least three times. At the end of your workout, spend about two minutes repeating some of these stretches.

▶ **Sit-and-Reach Stretch**
HINT—Remember to bend at the waist. Keep your eyes on your toes!

◀ **Hurdler's Stretch**
HINT—Keep the toes of your extended leg pointed up.

▶ **Upper-Back and Shoulder Stretch** HINT—Try to stretch your hand down so that it rests flat against your back.

▼ Thigh Stretch HINT— Keep both hands flat on the ground. Lean as far forward as you can.

► Calf Stretch HINT—Keep both feet on the floor during this stretch. Try changing the distance between your feet. Is the stretch better for you when your legs are closer together or farther apart?

▼ Shoulder and Chest Stretch HINT—Pulling your hands slowly toward the floor gives a better stretch. Keep your elbows straight, but not locked!

Tips for Stretching

- Never bounce when stretching.

- Hold each stretch for fifteen to twenty seconds.

- Breathe normally. This helps your body get the oxygen it needs.

- Do NOT stretch until it hurts. Stretch only until you feel a slight pull.

Health and Safety Handbook

Being Physically Active

The President's Challenge

The President's Challenge is a physical fitness program designed for students ages 6 to 17. It's made up of five activities that promote physical fitness. Each participant receives an emblem patch and a certificate signed by the President.

The Five Awards

 Presidential Physical Fitness Award—presented to students scoring in the top 15 percent in all events.

 National Physical Fitness Award—presented to students scoring in the top 50 percent in all events.

 Health Fitness Award—awarded to all other participants.

 Participant Physical Fitness Award—presented to students who complete all items but score below the top 50 percent in one or more items.

 Active Lifestyle Award—recognizes students who participate in daily physical activity of any type for five days per week, 60 minutes a day, or 11,000 pedometer steps for six weeks.

The five activities

1. Curl-Ups or Sit-Ups measure abdominal muscle strength.

- Lie on the floor with your arms across your chest and your legs bent. Have a partner hold your feet.

- Lift your upper body off the ground, and then lower it until it just touches the floor.

- Repeat as many times as you can in one minute.

© Harcourt

2. Shuttle Run measures leg strength and endurance.

- Run to the blocks and pick one up.

- Bring it back to the starting line.

- Repeat with the other block.

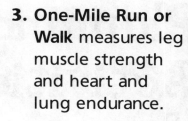

3. One-Mile Run or Walk measures leg muscle strength and heart and lung endurance.

- Run or walk a mile as fast as you can.

4. Pull-Ups measure the strength and endurance of arm and shoulder muscles.

- Hang by your hands from a bar.

- Pull your body up until your chin is over the bar. Lower your body again without touching the floor.

- Repeat as many times as you can.

5. V-Sit Reach measures the flexibility of your legs and back.

- Sit on the floor with your feet behind the line.

- Reach forward as far as you can.

© Harcourt

Being Physically Active

Planning Your Weekly Activities

Being active every day is important for your overall health. Physical activity helps you manage stress, maintain a healthful weight, and strengthen your body systems. The Activity Pyramid, like MyPyramid, can help you make a variety of choices in the right amounts to keep your body strong and healthy.

The Activity Pyramid

Sitting Still
Watching television, playing computer games
Small Amounts of Time

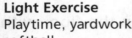

Light Exercise
Playtime, yardwork, softball
2–3 times a week

Strength and Flexibility Exercises
Weight training, dancing, pull-ups
2–3 times a week

Aerobic Exercises
Biking, running, soccer, hiking
30+ minutes, 2–3 times a week

Regular Activities
Walking to school, taking the stairs, helping with housework
Every day

First Aid

For Bleeding—Universal Precautions

You can get some diseases from another person's blood. Avoid touching anyone's blood. To treat a wound, follow the steps below.

If someone else is bleeding

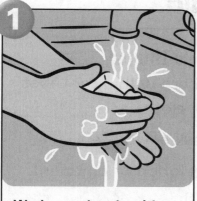

1 Wash your hands with soap if possible.

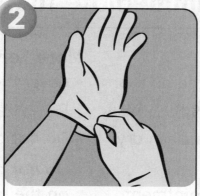

2 Put on protective gloves, if available.

3 Wash small wounds with water. Do not wash serious wounds.

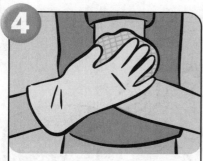

4 Place a clean gauze pad or cloth over the wound. Press firmly for ten minutes. Don't lift the gauze during this time.

5 If you don't have gloves, have the injured person hold the gauze or cloth in place with his or her hand.

6 If after ten minutes the bleeding has stopped, bandage the wound. If the bleeding has not stopped, continue pressing on the wound and get help.

If you are bleeding, you do not need to avoid your own blood.

For Burns

- Minor burns are called first-degree burns and involve only the top layer of skin. The skin is red and dry, and the burn is painful.

- Second-degree burns cause deeper damage. The burns cause blisters, redness, swelling, and pain.

- Third-degree burns are the most serious because they damage all layers of the skin. The skin is usually white or charred black. The area may feel numb because the nerve endings have been destroyed.

All burns need immediate first aid.

Minor Burns

- Run cool water over the burn or soak it for at least five minutes.

- Cover the burn with a clean dry bandage.

- Do *not* put lotion or ointment on the burn.

More Serious Burns

- Cover the burn with a cool, wet bandage or cloth.

- Do *not* break any blisters.

- Do *not* put lotion or ointment on the burn.

- Get help from an adult right away.

For Nosebleeds

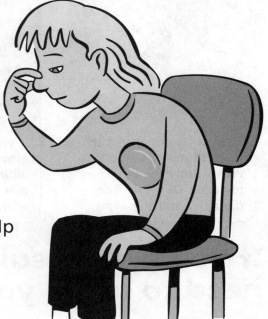

- Sit down, and tilt your head forward. Pinch your nostrils together for at least ten minutes.

- You can also put a cloth-covered cold pack on the bridge of your nose.

- If your nose continues to bleed, get help from an adult.

© Harcourt

For Choking

If someone else is choking

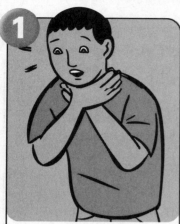

1 Recognize the Universal Choking Sign—grasping the throat with both hands. This sign means a person is choking and needs help.

2 Stand behind the choking person, and put your arms around his or her waist. Place your fist above the person's navel. Grab your fist with your other hand.

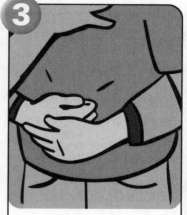

3 Pull your hands toward yourself, and give five quick, hard, upward thrusts on the person's stomach.

If you are choking when alone

1 Make a fist, and place it above your navel. Grab your fist with your other hand. Pull your hands up with a quick, hard thrust.

2 Or, keep your hands on your belly, lean your body over the back of a chair or over a counter, and shove your fist in and up.

© Harcourt

Health and Safety Handbook　　　　　　　**Teaching Resources • 101**

For Dental Emergencies

You should know what to do if you have a dental emergency.

Broken Tooth

- Rinse your mouth with warm water. Wrap a cold pack with a cloth. Place it on the injured area. Save any parts of the broken tooth. Call your dentist immediately.

Knocked-Out Permanent Tooth

- Find the tooth and clean it carefully. Handle it by the top (crown), not the root. Put it back into the socket if you can. Hold it in place by biting on clean cloth. If the tooth cannot be put back in, place it in a cup with milk or water. See a dentist immediately. Time is very important in saving the tooth.

Bitten Tongue or Lip

- Apply pressure to the bleeding area with a cloth. Use a cold pack covered with a cloth to stop swelling. If the bleeding doesn't stop within 15 minutes, go to a hospital emergency room.

Food/Objects Caught Between Teeth

- Use dental floss to gently take out the object. Never use anything sharp to take out an object that is stuck between your teeth. If it cannot be removed, call your dentist.

© Harcourt

For Insect Bites and Stings

- Always tell an adult about bites and stings.

- Scrape out the stinger with your fingernail.

- Wash the area with soap and water.

- A covered ice cube or cold pack will usually take away the pain from insect bites. A paste made from baking soda and water also helps.

- If the bite or sting is more serious and is on an arm or leg, keep the leg or arm dangling down. Apply a cold, wet cloth. Get help immediately.

- If you find a tick on your skin, remove it. Protect your fingers with a tissue or cloth to prevent contact with infectious tick fluids. If you must use your bare hands, wash them right away.

- If the tick has already bitten you, ask an adult to remove it. Using tweezers, an adult should grab the tick as close to your skin as possible and pull the tick out in one steady motion. Do not use petroleum jelly because it may cause the tick to struggle releasing its infectious fluids. Wash the bite site.

For Skin Rashes from Plants

Many poisonous plants have three leaves. Remember, " Leaves of three, let them be." If you touch a poisonous plant, wash the area and your hands. If a rash develops, follow these tips.

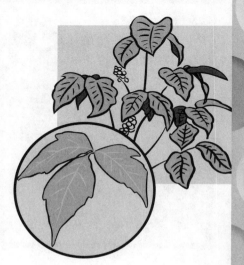

- Apply calamine lotion or a baking soda and water paste. Try not to scratch. Tell an adult.

- If you get blisters, do not pop them. If they burst, keep the area clean and dry. If your rash does not go away in two weeks, or if the rash is on your face or in your eyes, see your doctor.

© Harcourt

Health and Safety Handbook

Teaching Resources • 103

Alcohol, Tobacco, and Other Drugs
A Drug-Free School

Many schools make rules and sponsor activities to encourage people to say *no* to drugs. This makes the school a more healthful environment for everyone.

School Rules

Many schools decide to be drug free. They often have strict penalties for anyone found with drugs. For example, a person found with drugs may be expelled or suspended from school.

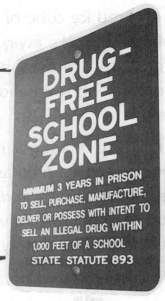

Positive Peer Pressure

Peer pressure can be bad or good. *Positive peer pressure* is people the same age encouraging each other to make healthful choices. For example, students may make posters or hold rallies to encourage others not to use drugs.

Alcohol, Tobacco, and Other Drugs

What to Do When Others Use Drugs

You should make a personal commitment not to use alcohol, tobacco, or other drugs. But you may be around other students or adults who make unhealthful choices about drugs. Here is what you can do.

Know the Signs

Someone who has a problem with drugs may be sad or angry all the time, skip school or work, or forget events often.

Talk to a Trusted Adult

Do not keep someone's drug use a secret. Ask a trusted adult for help. You can also get support from adults to help you resist pressure to use drugs.

Be Supportive

If a person decides to stop using drugs, help the person quit. Suggest healthful activities you can do together. Tell the person you are happy he or she has quit.

Stay Healthy

Do not stay anywhere that drugs are being used. If you cannot leave, stay as far away from the drugs as possible.

Where to Get Help

- Hospitals
- Alateen
- Alcoholics Anonymous
- Narcotics Anonymous
- Al-Anon
- Drug treatment centers

© Harcourt

Backpack Safety

Carrying a backpack that is too heavy can injure your back. Carrying one incorrectly also can hurt you.

Safe Weight

A full backpack should weigh no more than 10 to 15 percent of your body weight. Less is better. To find 10 percent, divide your body weight by 10. Here are some examples:

Your Weight (pounds)	Maximum Backpack Weight (pounds)
60	6
65	$6\frac{1}{2}$
70	7

This is the right way to carry a backpack.

Safe Use

- Use a pack with wide shoulder straps and a padded back.

- Lighten your load. Leave unnecessary items at home.

- Pack heavier items inside the pack so that they will be closest to your back.

- Always use both shoulder straps to carry the pack.

- Never wear a backpack while riding a bicycle. The weight makes it harder to stay balanced. Use the bicycle basket or saddlebags instead.

This is the wrong way to carry a backpack.

© Harcourt

Bike Safety Check

A safe bike should be the right size for you.

- You should be able to rest your heel on the pedal when you sit on your bike with the pedal in the lowest position.

- When you are standing astride your bike with both feet flat on the ground, your body should be 2 inches above the bar that goes from the handlebar to the seat.

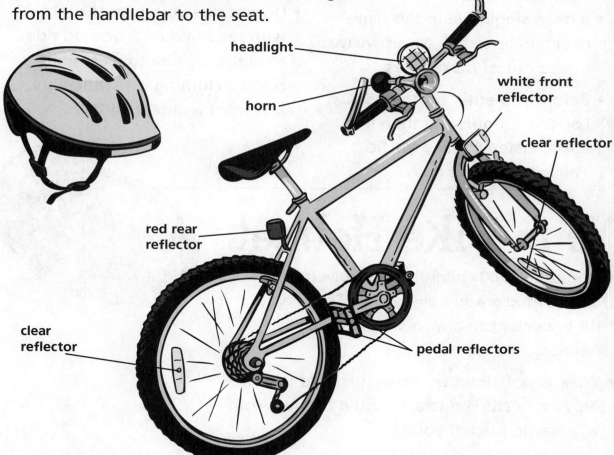

headlight

horn

white front reflector

clear reflector

red rear reflector

clear reflector

pedal reflectors

A bike should have all the safety equipment shown above. Does *your* bike pass the test?

Health and Safety
Safety While Riding

Here are some tips for safe bicycle riding.

- Always wear your bike helmet, even for short distances.

- Check your bike every time you ride it. Is it in safe working condition?

- Ride in single file in the same direction as traffic. Never weave in and out of parked cars.

- Before you enter a street, **STOP**. **Look** left, right, and then left again. **Listen** for any traffic. **Think** before you go.

- Walk your bike across an intersection. **Look** left, right, and then left again. Wait for traffic to pass.

- Obey all traffic signs and signals.

- Do not ride your bike at night without an adult. If you do ride at night, be sure to wear light-colored clothing, use reflectors, and front and rear lights.

Your Bike Helmet

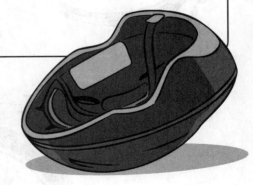

- About 500,000 children are involved in bike-related crashes every year. That's why it's important to always wear your bike helmet.

- Wear your helmet properly. It should lie flat on your head. The straps should be snug so it will stay in place if you fall.

- If you do fall and your helmet hits the ground, replace it—even if it doesn't look damaged. The inner foam lining may be crushed. It might not protect you if you fell again.

Health and Safety

Storm Safety

- **In a Tornado** Take cover in a sheltered area away from doors and windows. An interior hallway or basement is best. Stay in the shelter until the danger has passed.

- **In a Hurricane** Prepare for high winds by securing objects outside or bringing them indoors. Cover windows and glass with plywood. Listen to weather bulletins for instructions. If asked to evacuate, proceed to emergency shelters.

- **In a Winter Storm or Blizzard** Stock up on food that does not have to be cooked. Dress in thin layers that help trap the body's heat. Pay special attention to the head and neck. If you are caught in a vehicle, turn on the dome light to make the vehicle visible to search crews.

Earthquake Safety

An earthquake is a strong shaking or sliding of the ground. The tips below can help you and your family stay safe in an earthquake.

Before an Earthquake
- Attach tall, heavy furniture, such as bookcases, to the wall. Store the heaviest items on the lowest shelves.
- Check for fire risks. An adult should bolt down gas appliances, and use flexible hosing and connections for both gas and water lines.
- An adult should strengthen and anchor overhead light fixtures to help keep them from falling.

During an Earthquake
- If you are outdoors, stay there and move away from buildings and utility wires.
- If you are indoors, take cover under a heavy desk or table, or in a doorway. Stay away from glass doors and windows and from heavy objects that might fall.
- If you are in a car, have the driver go to an open area away from buildings and overpasses.

After an Earthquake
- Keep watching for falling objects as aftershocks shake the area.
- Check for hidden structural problems.
- Check for broken gas, electric, and water lines. If you smell gas, shut off the gas main. Leave the area. Report the leak.

© Harcourt

Summer and Backyard Safety

Use this list to check for hazards before playing in your backyard or your friends' backyards.

- **Poison** Many common plants are poisonous. Find out which plants in your area are poisonous. Use caution around yard chemicals, such as fertilizers, pesticides, pool chemicals, and pet products.

- **Fire** Be careful around barbecue grills, lighter fluid, and bonfires. Fires can get out of hand very quickly, and accidents can happen before anyone realizes what is happening.

- **Water** Always swim where lifeguards are on duty. Use a life jacket when boating. Wear boat shoes around wet and slippery decks.

- **Cutting Tools and Power Tools** Treat lawn mowers and all power tools with respect. Never leave them unattended where a child might turn them on.

- **Strangling Hazards** Use caution around fences, decks, and stairway railings. Clotheslines and rope can also be hazardous if someone gets caught in them.

- **Falling** Remember to use good sense and good manners around climbing bars, ladders, and tree houses. Pushing or shoving a person can cause cuts, broken bones, and knocked-out teeth.

- **Insects and Other Animals** Ticks, mosquitoes, bees, or other flying insects can cause diseases or bites that can be fatal. Strange dogs wandering into your backyard should be considered dangerous and avoided.

- **Sun** Use sunscreen, wear a hat, and drink plenty of liquids when out in the sun.

Health and Safety

Family Emergency Plan

By having a plan, your family can protect itself during an emergency. To make an emergency plan, your family needs to gather information, make some choices, and practice parts of the plan.

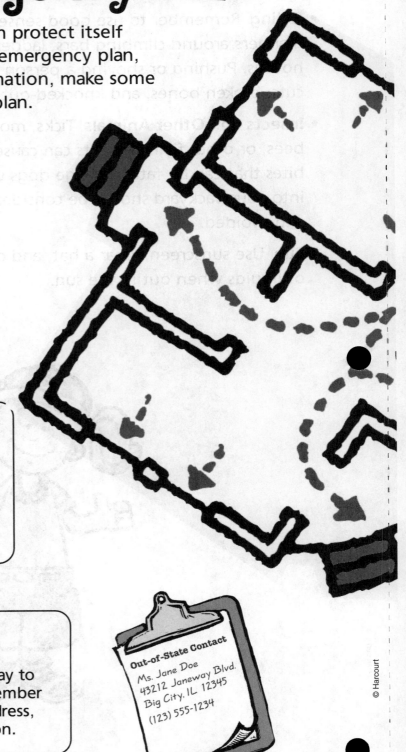

Know What Could Happen

Learn the possible emergencies in your area, such as fires, storms, earthquakes, or floods. List the possible emergencies.

Have Two Meeting Places

Pick two places to meet. One place should be within a block of your home. The second place should be farther away—for example, the main door to your school.

Know Your Family Contact

Choose someone who lives far away to be a contact person. Each family member should memorize the full name, address, and telephone number of the person.

Out-of-State Contact
Ms. Jane Doe
43212 Janeway Blvd.
Big City, IL 12345
(123) 555-1234

© Harcourt

Practice Evacuating

During a fire, you need to evacuate, or get out of, your home right away. Use your list of possible emergencies to plan how to evacuate. Practice evacuating at least twice a year.

▼ This woman is showing her daughter how to turn off the main water valve at their home.

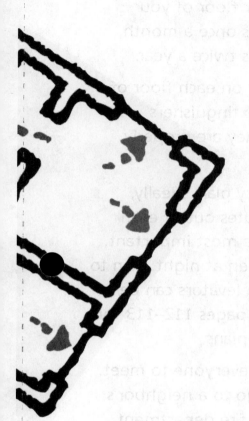

Learn How to Turn Off Utilities

Water, electricity, and gas are *utilities*. Some emergencies may break utilities or make them dangerous. With an adult's help, learn when and how to turn off utilities. **CAUTION:** If you turn off the gas, a professional must turn it back on.

▲ outdoor water shut-off valve

Make an Emergency Supply Kit

After an emergency, your family may need first-aid supplies or food. Your family can use a checklist from the American Red Cross or another disaster group to make an emergency supply kit.

© Harcourt

Fire Safety

Fires cause more deaths than any other type of disaster. But a fire doesn't have to be deadly if you and your family prepare your home and follow some basic safety rules.

- Install smoke detectors outside sleeping areas and on every other floor of your home. Test the detectors once a month, and change the batteries twice a year.

- Keep a fire extinguisher on each floor of your home. Check the extinguishers monthly to make sure they are properly charged.

- Make a family emergency plan. Ideally, there should be two routes out of each room. Sleeping areas are most important, because most fires happen at night. Plan to use stairs only, because elevators can be dangerous in a fire. See pages 112–113 for more about emergency plans.

- Pick a place outside for everyone to meet. Choose one person to go to a neighbor's home to call 911 or the fire department.

- Practice crawling low to avoid smoke.

- If your clothes catch fire, follow the three steps shown here.

1. STOP

2. DROP

3. ROLL

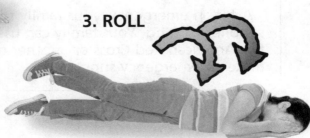

© Harcourt

Good Posture at the Computer

Good posture is important when using a computer. To help prevent eyestrain, stress, and injuries, follow the posture tips shown below. Also, remember to grasp the mouse lightly and take frequent breaks for stretching.

top of screen at or just below eye level

shoulders in line with ears and hips

neck and shoulders relaxed

wrists straight

arms at sides, bent as shown

feet flat on floor

© Harcourt

Safety near Water

Water can be very dangerous. A person can drown in five minutes or less. The best way to be safe near water is to learn how to swim. You should also follow these rules:

- Never swim without the supervision of a lifeguard or a responsible adult.

- If you cannot swim, stay in shallow water. Do not use a blow-up raft to go into deep water.

- Know the rules for the beach or pool and obey them. Do not run or shove others while you are near the water.

- Never dive in head-first the first time. Go feet-first instead to learn how deep the water is.

Pool Rules

1. Public use of pool is permitted only when a lifeguard is on duty.

2. All patrons must shower before entering the pool.

3. No food, drink, gum, glass, or smoking in the pool or on the deck.

4. No animals in pool or on pool deck.

5. Children under the age of 8 years of age must be accompanied by an adult guardian (age 18 or older). Children under 6 years of age must be accompanied by an adult in the water. THIS INCLUDES THE PLAY POOL.

6. Inappropriate behavior such as horseplay, fighting, or use of abusive language is not permitted.

7. Running is not allowed anywhere in pool area.

8. Diving from the side of the pool in the shallow area is not allowed.

9. Flips or back dives from the side of the pool are not allowed.

10. Only one person at a time is allowed on the diving board. Only one bounce is allowed on the diving board.

11. Only Coast Guard-approved flotation devices may be used in the pool.

12. Use of mask, fins, or snorkel is prohibited.

13. Loitering or playing in or around the locker rooms, showers, or restrooms is not allowed.

14. Only regular, clean bathing suits may be worn. Street clothes are not allowed in the pool.

15. Pool capacity and pool hours are posted at the office.

Protect your skin with sunscreen with an SPF of at least 30. Protect your eyes with sunglasses.

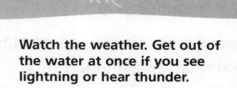

Watch the weather. Get out of the water at once if you see lightning or hear thunder.

Wear a Coast Guard–approved life jacket anytime you are in a boat. Wear one when you ride a personal watercraft, too. Know what to do in an emergency.

© Harcourt

Health and Safety

When Home Alone

Everyone stays home alone sometimes. When you stay home alone, it's important to know how to take care of yourself. Here are some easy rules to follow that will help keep you safe when you are home by yourself.

Do These Things

- Lock all the doors and windows. Be sure you know how to lock and unlock all the locks.

- If someone who is nasty or mean calls, hang up immediately. Tell an adult about the call when he or she gets home. Your parents may not want you to answer the phone at all.

- If you have an emergency, call 911. Be prepared to describe the problem and to give your full name, address, and telephone number. Follow all instructions given to you. Do not hang up the phone until you are told to do so.

- If you see anyone hanging around outside your home, call a neighbor or the police.

- If you see or smell smoke, go outside right away. If you live in an apartment, do not take the elevator. Go to a neighbor's house, and call 911 immediately.

- Entertain yourself. Time will pass more quickly if you are not bored. Work on a hobby, read a book or magazine, do your homework, or clean your room. Before you know it, an adult will be home.

© Harcourt

Health and Safety Handbook

Do NOT Do These Things

- Do NOT use the stove, microwave, or oven unless an adult family member has given you permission, and you know how to use these appliances.

- Do NOT open the door for anyone you don't know or for anyone who is not supposed to be in your home.

- Do NOT talk to strangers on the telephone. Do not tell anyone that you are home alone. If the call is for an adult family member, say that he or she can't come to the phone right now and take a message.

- Do NOT have friends over unless you have permission from your parents or other adult family members.

A telephone with caller ID display can help you decide whether to answer the phone.

© Harcourt

Health and Safety
Safety on the Internet

You can use the Internet for fun, education, research, and more. But like anything else, you should use the Internet with caution. Some people compare the Internet to a real city—not all the people there are people you want to meet, and not all the places you can go are places you want to be. Just like in a real city, you have to use common sense and follow safety rules to protect yourself. Below are some easy rules to follow to help you stay safe online.

Rules for Online Safety

- Talk with an adult family member to set up rules for going online. Decide what time of day you can go online, how long you can be online, and appropriate places you can visit. Do not access other areas or break the rules you establish.

- Don't give out information such as your name, address, telephone number, your picture, or the name or location of your school.

- If you find any information online that makes you uncomfortable or if you receive a message that is mean or makes you feel uncomfortable, tell an adult family member right away.

- Never agree to meet anyone in person. If you want to get together with someone you meet online, check with an adult family member first. If a meeting is approved, arrange to meet in a public place and take an adult with you.

Activity Book Answer Key • Chapter 1

Your Amazing Body

Quick Study
Pages 1–2

Lesson 1

Summary: skeletal system; muscular system; nervous system

Lesson Details: skeletal system, nervous system; nerves, brain; muscular system, tendons

Lesson 2

Summary: lungs, respiratory system, stomach, intestines, digestive system

Lesson Details: Each system takes something into the body and changes it to a form the body can use. Each system has a way of getting rid of wastes.

Lesson 3

Summary: life cycle

Lesson Details: Check student's drawings and sentences.

Lesson 4

Summary: cells

Lesson Details: tissues, organs, organ system

Lesson 5

Summary: habits

Lesson Details: protects your body from injury, washing hands, visiting doctor, makes sure your teeth are healthy

Reading Skill
Page 3

Main Idea: Your muscular system is made up of three kinds of muscles.

Detail:
- Muscles that are attached to your bones
- Cause movements you control
- Help you walk, chew, and sing

Detail:
- Muscles that cause movements you do not control
- Help move blood, digest food, and make lungs work

Detail:
- Muscle that is found only in your heart
- Controls heartbeat
- Not under your control

Problem Solving
Page 4

A. Possible answer: Tashia can talk with her parents to find out why they do not trust her to go alone. After listening to her parents, Tashia may realize that her parents do trust her. The problem is that they do not trust the strangers she may meet on the way to the pool.

B. Possible answers: Wendell can tell his mom that a dog would not be a lot of work. He can talk to her and find out exactly what she is worried about. He can show her that he is responsible by caring for some fish first. If he takes good care of the fish, his mom will see that he is responsible.

Vocabulary Reinforcement
Page 5

A. 1. digestive system
    2. mouth
    3. esophagus
    4. stomach
    5. small intestine
    6. liver
    7. large intestine
B. 8. Bones
    9. diaphragm
    10. growth rate

© Harcourt

Activity Book Answer Key • Chapter 2

Taking Care of Yourself

Quick Study
Pages 6–7

Lesson 1
Summary: pores, bacteria, sunscreen
Lesson Details: tiny hairs, pores; Wash with soap and water. Use sunscreen.

Lesson 2
Summary: plaque, cavity, dental floss, Fluoride
Lesson Details: Answers should reflect the steps provided in the text.

Lesson 3
Summary: ear canal, eardrum
Lesson Details: Turn the sound down on your own CD player or TV. Keep the outer parts of your ears clean. Never put anything inside your ear canal.

Lesson 4
Summary: consumer
Lesson Details: Possible answers: Know how to read the product label. Compare prices. Compare ingredients.

Lesson 5
Summary: advertising
Lesson Details: Possible answers: show happy people using the product, use catchy tunes, use bright colors or pictures in packaging, use a famous person

Reading Skill
Page 8
Possible answer: You need to care for your skin and teeth every day. Use soap to wash your hands before you eat and after you use the bathroom. Bathe or shower whenever you are dirty or sweaty. Put on sunscreen whenever you are in the sun. Brush your teeth at least twice a day. Floss at least once a day.

Problem Solving
Page 9
A. Possible answer: Nicole could set a goal to clean her teeth at certain times while camping. For example, she could plan to floss and brush her teeth first thing after breakfast each morning and again after dinner each night.
B. Possible answer: Alton could set a goal to use sources other than advertisements for product information. He might ask his doctor or other trusted adults for advice.

Vocabulary Reinforcement
Page 10
A. 1. ear canal
   2. consumer
   3. plaque
   4. bacteria
   5. pores
   6. eardrum
   7. cavity
   8. advertisements
   9. fluoride
B. Check students' sentences.

Food for a Healthy Body

Quick Study
Pages 11–12

| Lesson 1 |

Summary: nutrients, nutrition, diet
Lesson Details:
  2. vitamins
  3. proteins
  4. minerals
  5. fats
  6. water
[these answers can be in any order]

| Lesson 2 |

Summary: MyPyramid, balanced diet
Lesson Details: Possible answers: carrots, radishes, broccoli [accept any vegetable]

Possible answers: apples, oranges, strawberries [accept any fruit]

| Lesson 3 |

Summary: snacks
Lesson Details: potato chips, candy bar, and cookies should be crossed out

| Lesson 4 |

Summary: ingredients, label
Lesson Details: Compare nutrition facts.
Compare unit prices.
[these answers can be in either order]

| Lesson 5 |

Summary: spoiled
Lesson Details: frozen foods
meats, chicken, and eggs
fruits and vegetables
[this order only]

Reading Skill
Page 13
Possible answers:
Alike
Both are among the six basic nutrients.
Both are parts of a balanced diet.
Both give your body energy.
Different
proteins: help your body grow
good sources of proteins: some foods from the Meat and Beans group
good sources of carbohydrates: some foods from the Grains group

Problem Solving
Page 14
A. Possible answer: Tim should choose the carrots. They are a crunchy, healthful snack. If Tim chooses carrots, he will follow his family's rules and have the crunchy snack. Yogurt is healthful, but is not crunchy, so it would not be the best choice.
B. No, Deshawn did not make the best choice. Possible explanation: A candy bar will not give the nutrition he needs for playing soccer. Deshawn should not choose candy just because it is what his teammates are eating.

Vocabulary Reinforcement
Page 15
1. B
2. F
3. D
4. H
5. fluoride
6. nutrients
7. diet
8. ingredients
9. MyPyramid

© Harcourt

Activity Book Answer Key • Chapter 4

Activity for a Healthy Body

Quick Study
Pages 16–17

Lesson 1
Summary: exercise, strength, flexibility, endurance, aerobic exercise

Lesson Details: Possible answers: take the stairs, help with housework

Possible answers: watch television, play computer games

Possible answers: biking, running, soccer, hiking

Lesson 2
Summary: warm-up, cool-down, safety gear, mouth guard

Lesson Details: Stand near a wall. Keep both feet flat on the floor. Stretch the calf.

Thigh stretch.

Place your hands behind your back. Join hands. Pull your hands toward the floor.

Lesson 3
Summary: ten, sleep

Lesson Details:

Babies	16
Children	10
Teens	9
Adults	10

Reading Skill
Page 18

Possible answers:

I feel good.

I am flexible.

I am strong.

My heart is healthy.

My lungs hold a lot of air.

I am in a good mood.

I have a lot of endurance.

Problem Solving
Page 19

A. Possible answers: No, Tim did not make a healthful decision. Your body loses water when you exercise. It is important to drink water before, during, and after exercise. Tim should have asked an adult to help him get some water for practice.

B. Possible answer: Maria should keep trying. Sometimes you can't meet a health goal right away. It is important to keep trying.

Vocabulary Reinforcement
Page 20

A. 1. flexibility
2. exercise
3. strength
4. endurance
5. aerobic exercise

B. Check students' sentences.

Activity Book Answer Key • Chapter 5

Keeping Safe

Quick Study
Pages 21–22

Lesson 1

Summary: safety rules, hazard, injury, passenger, limit

Lesson Details: Possible answer: I am a person responsible for keeping myself safe, because I can choose to follow the safety rules and limits set by my family, teachers, school, and community.

Lesson 2

Summary: stranger, bully, trusted adult

Lesson Details: Check students' answers.

Lesson 3

Summary: injury

Lesson Details: Carry only one person. Place your backpack in the basket. Wear reflective clothing. Ride only in daylight. Walk across streets.

Reading Skill
Page 23

What I Read: Tamika's parents have told her to be extra careful with her new backpack.

What I Know: Tamika's parents are likely to be more concerned about her safety than her backpack.

Conclusion: Tamika should slip out of her backpack, leave it behind, and run as fast as she can to a safe place or to a trusted adult.

Problem Solving
Page 24

A. Possible answers: Tasha can take homework with her and leave with Jordan in the morning. Jordan can take homework with him and wait for Tasha in the afternoon. Alternatively, one or both children might arrange for a ride from a teammate's parent.

B. Possible answer: If the boys decide that each will decorate one wall in the room with his choice of posters or photographs, the decision will be fair to both.

Vocabulary Reinforcement
Page 25

A. **Across**
   3. limit
   5. passenger
   6. hazard
   Down
   1. bully
   2. stranger
   4. injury

B. Check students' sentences. Possible answer: A broken streetlight is a hazard that could lead to an injury.

Activity Book Answer Key • Chapter 6

Emergency Safety

Quick Study
Pages 26–27

Lesson 1

Summary: emergency, poison
Lesson Details:
stop, drop, roll to put out the fire

Lesson 2

Summary: electricity
Lesson Details:
F; Hold the plug to unplug an appliance.
F; Never touch another person's blood.
T
F; Scrape out insect stingers.
T

Lesson 3

Summary: disaster
Lesson Details:
1. underline first sentence; cross out second sentence; A tornado can break glass and destroy homes.
2. underline first sentence; cross out second sentence; An earthquake can cause things to fall on you.
3. cross out first sentence; underline second sentence; A hurricane can break glass and flood your home.
4. cross out first sentence; underline second sentence; Lightning can enter a house through water pipes.

Reading Skill
Page 28
Sequence boxes:
1. Make a floor plan of your home.
2. Draw arrows to show two ways out of each room.
3. Decide on a meeting place outside your home.
4. Decide how often to practice the plan.

Problem Solving
Page 29
A. Possible answer: Kia could tell Angie that she wants her to be safe. She could explain why they both should go inside. Kia can listen to what Angie wants to play inside.
B. Possible answer: Students should recognize that Lee may have injured himself even if he says he is OK now. Matt should tell the teacher on duty exactly what happened. The boys should do what the teacher tells them to do.

Vocabulary Reinforcement
Page 30
1. DISASTER
2. POISON
3. ELECTRICITY
4. EMERGENCY
Secret Message: TELL AN ADULT

Activity Book Answer Key • Chapter 7

Preventing Disease

Quick Study
Pages 31–32

Lesson 1

Summary: symptom, disease

Lesson Details: Possible answers: fever, sore throat, headache

[these answers can be in any order]

Lesson 2

Summary: communicable disease, pathogens, bacteria, viruses

Lesson Details: virus, bacteria

Lesson 3

Summary: immunity, vaccine, medicine

Lesson Details: Possible answers: You can't receive treatment for an illness unless an adult knows about your symptoms. Some illnesses must be treated with medicine, and you need an adult's help to take medicine.

Lesson 4

Summary: noncommunicable disease; diabetes, cancer [in either order]

Lesson Details: Possible answers: sneezing, watery eyes, itchy rash

Possible answers: coughing, difficulty breathing

Lesson 5

Summary: abstinence

Lesson Details: Possible answers: Eat healthful foods. Get exercise. Avoid tobacco.

Reading Skill
Page 33

1. Bacteria get into your body.
2. Bacteria make more bacteria.
3. You feel symptoms.
4. Tell a parent about your symptoms.
5. A parent can check your symptoms.
6. You get medicine or go to a doctor.

Problem Solving
Page 34

A. Possible answer: Tom could ride his bike each day, take a long walk, or play basketball with friends. Exercise reduces stress and may help Tom's body fight off disease.

B. Possible answer: Heather already knows she is stressed, and she knows why. She should talk to her parents or a trusted friend about the way she is feeling. She should visualize herself doing well at the soccer play-offs.

Vocabulary Reinforcement
Page 35

1. virus
2. Abstinence
3. noncommunicable diseases
4. vaccine
5. disease
6. Cancer
7. bacteria
8. communicable disease
9. Immunity
10. pathogens

© Harcourt

Activity Book Answer Key • Chapter 8

Medicines and Other Drugs

Quick Study
Pages 36–37

Lesson 1

Summary: Drugs, caffeine, medicines, over-the-counter medicines, prescription medicines, side effect

Lesson Details:

over-the-counter medicine —————— iced tea

item with caffeine —————— drug from a doctor

prescription medicine —————— antibiotic cream

Lesson 2

Summary: safety rules, medicine label

Lesson Details:

Any three of the following are possible responses: Never take a medicine on your own. Follow the directions on the label exactly. Tell an adult if you have side effects. Never share medicine or use someone else's medicine. Don't use old medicines. Keep medicines on high shelves in locked cabinets. Keep medicines away from small children.

Lesson 3

Summary: inhalants; marijuana; cocaine

Lesson Details:

inhalants: violent behavior, brain damage, death
marijuana: breathing problems, get sick more often
cocaine: lung or brain damage, stroke, heart attack, death

Lesson 4

Summary: refuse

Lesson Details: You can go to jail for using drugs; drugs change the way your brain works so you can't think well; drugs can cause accidents, illness, and even death.

Any three of the following possible ways: ignoring the person offering drugs; changing the subject; suggesting something else to do; walking away; saying *no* and turning away

Reading Skill
Page 38

1. **What I Know:** If you don't take medicine the way it is prescribed, it might not work.
   Conclusion: Mr. Janow might still be sick because he did not take the medicine the way he was supposed to take it.

2. **What I Read:** Marcy's mother got her medicine for her cough and used it the way the directions said to use it.
   Conclusion: Since Marcy's mom followed the directions, the medicine worked and Marcy's cough went away.

Problem Solving
Page 39

A. Possible answer: Alan could tell Chris, "No, sniffing glue is dangerous." Then Alan could say he has heard of people being poisoned from sniffing inhalants. He could say, "I don't want to lose any brain cells, thanks." Then he could ask Chris if he wants to play a game instead.

B. Possible answer: Jessie can first say *no* and tell Mary that she doesn't like any kind of smoking. She could tell Amber that marijuana can make you sick. She could say, "I just don't want to do that." Then Jessie could offer to go biking with Amber.

Vocabulary Reinforcement
Page 40

A. 1. marijuana
   2. side effect
   3. antibiotic
   4. medicines
   5. inhalants
   6. safety rules
   7. caffeine
   8. cocaine
   9. prescriptions

B. Just say *no, sir!*

Activity Book Answer Key • Chapter 9

Avoiding Tobacco and Alcohol

Quick Study
Pages 41–42

Lesson 1

Summary: smokeless tobacco, chewing tobacco, tar, nicotine, addiction, cancer, environmental tobacco smoke

Lesson Details:

Mouth: bad breath, stains teeth, gums and lips crack and bleed, mouth cancer

Throat: cough, throat cancer

Heart: heart beats fast, blood vessels shrink, heart disease

Lungs: hard to breathe, lung cancer, other lung diseases

Lesson 2

Summary: Alcohol, alcoholism

Lesson Details: Possible answers: Alcohol can affect speech and how a person moves or sees; alcohol can cause the brain to shut down; alcohol can cause liver damage and failure and even death; alcohol can cause your personality to change; alcohol use can cause an upset stomach and even damage the stomach.

Lesson 3

Summary: refuse, laws

Lesson Details: Possible answers: Look surprised and say, "That's against the law." Say *no* and walk away. Say, "I've promised my parents not to do that." Laugh and say, "I want to have fun, not hurt my body." Look at a clock and say, "I have to get going."

Reading Skill
Page 43

Main Idea: Using tobacco can cause health problems.

Detail: hurt throat and mouth, including cancer, coughs, cracked lips, and bad breath

Detail: risks to heart, such as smaller blood vessels, heart beating faster and harder, and heart disease

Detail: lung problems, including breathing hard, lung cancer, and other lung diseases

Problem Solving
Page 44

A. Possible answers: Janice can first say *no*. She can tell her friends that smoking can make you sick and she doesn't want to get sick. Then Janice can ask whether anyone wants to go with her to play the game four square. She can play the game with those friends and stay away from those who want to smoke.

B. Possible answers: Jack can tell Kevin *no*, that he doesn't want to try the alcohol because his parents would not like it if he tried drinking. "Besides," Jack can say, "that stuff can make you sick." Jack can tell Kevin he wants to go bike riding instead. If Kevin says *no*, Jack can shrug his shoulders, leave, and say, "See you around."

Vocabulary Reinforcement
Page 45

A.

1. f	6. b
2. c	7. d
3. i	8. e
4. g	9. h
5. a	10. j

B. Check students' sentences.

Activity Book Answer Key • Chapter 10

About Yourself and Others

Quick Study
Pages 46–47

Lesson 1

Summary: Emotions, needs, wants, self-control
Lesson Details: words, actions, body language; talking, exercising, or writing in a journal

Lesson 2

Summary: fear, stress
Lesson Details: Deshay probably feels grief. She should talk or write about her feelings.

Sam is probably angry. He can use an "I" message to tell his brother how he feels.

Lesson 3

Summary: Peers, peer pressure
Lesson Details:
with your family: Talk and listen; be helpful, caring, respectful

with a classmate who pressures you to do something wrong: Stand up for what you believe in without becoming angry.

Lesson 4

Summary: communicate, apologize
Lesson Details: Lines should be drawn as shown below.

First situation: I would apologize and ask my friend to forgive me.

Second situation: I would show compassion for my friend and treat her in a caring way.

Reading Skill
Page 48

First Effect: You may have a friend for life.
Second Effect: You feel good about yourself; you know you are stronger than peer pressure.

Problem Solving
Page 49

A. Possible answer: Katy feels stress because she has too much to do in a short time. She could tell Mary she can't ride with her today and will do it another time. Then she could tell her mom that she will clean her room after dinner so she can finish her homework now.

B. Possible answer: Jamal feels stress because he is afraid his friends will laugh at him when they find out that he is not a good player. Jamal could tell his friends the truth and admit that he really hasn't played much.

Vocabulary Reinforcement
Page 50

A. 1. c
2. b
3. g
4. h
5. a
6. e
7. d
8. f

B. Possible answer: You need to communicate your feelings to your peers.

Your Family and You

Quick Study
Pages 51–52

| Lesson 1 |

Summary: values
Lesson Details:

1. Ritual
2. Value
3. Value
4. Value
5. Ritual
6. Ritual
7. Ritual
8. Ritual
9. Value
10. Ritual
11. Value

| Lesson 2 |

Summary: divorce, sibling
Lesson Details: Talking about your feelings with your parents
E-mailing or writing a letter to a friend
Listening to how other family members feel

| Lesson 3 |

Summary: responsibilities, role
Lesson Details: Possible answers: setting the table, feeding a pet, doing homework, watering plants, cleaning his or her room

Reading Skill
Page 53

First paragraph possible answer—Main Ideas underlined in paragraph:

• Conflicts occur even when families get along well.
• Conflict is normal.
• work it out
• Communicating respectfully

Summary of paragraph:
Possible answer: Conflict happens when people have a disagreement and feelings get hurt. When there is conflict, it needs to be worked out. One way to do this is to use respectful communication.

Problem Solving
Page 54

A. Possible answer: Frank needs to tell Jamie that he is unhappy and that he needs his book. Jamie needs to listen to how her brother feels. Frank can offer to let his sister read the book when he is finished with it. Jamie needs to agree not to take Frank's things without asking him first.

B. Possible answer: Jason and Lucas both need to say how they feel by using "I" messages. Each also needs to listen to how the other feels. They could negotiate by spending part of their time together at the park and the rest of the time riding their bikes.

Vocabulary Reinforcement
Page 55

Across
3. values
5. responsibilities

Down
1. divorce
2. roles
4. sibling

Activity Book Answer Key • Chapter 12

Health in the Community

Quick Study
Pages 56–57

Lesson 1

Summary: community, health department, hospital, clinic

Lesson Details: Possible answers: give vaccinations; visit and care for people who are not able to leave home

Lesson 2

Summary: environment, pollution, noise pollution, air pollution

Lesson Details: car exhaust, tobacco smoke

Lesson 3

Summary: groundwater, water pollution

Lesson Details: 4, 2, 1, 3

Lesson 4

Summary: littering, reduce, reuse, recycle

Lesson Details: Reuse: Saves natural resources

Recycle: Saves money; reduces litter

Reading Skill
Page 58

Alike
- Both use gasoline.
- Both produce air pollution.

Different
- Hybrid cars use gas and electricity; regular cars use only gas.
- Hybrid cars produce less pollution.
- Hybrid cars use less gas.
- Hybrid cars are more expensive than regular cars.

Problem Solving
Page 59

A. Possible answer: The class can help the custodian clean up the mess. Then the class can make posters reminding students to dispose of their trash properly. The posters can be put up near the lunch area for the whole school to see.

B. Possible answer: Beth can contact her friends and ask if they would be willing to donate their outgrown clothing. Then she needs to find a place to collect and sort the clothing. She and her mother can set a date for the garage sale and post notices around the neighborhood, telling the date, place, and time of the sale.

Vocabulary Reinforcement
Page 60

1. c
2. f
3. g
4. b
5. d
6. j
7. i
8. a
9. k
10. m
11. e
12. h
13. l